IN SEARCH OF

Cover picture: *The Church of St Peter, Thorner.*

For Malcolm

In Search of Freedom

by
Diana Parsons

William Sessions Limited
York, England

ISBN 1 85072 295 1

Printed in 10½ on 11½ point Plantin Typeface
from Author's Disk
by Sessions of York
The Ebor Press
York, England

Contents

List of Illustrations

'In the future days, which we seek to make secure, we look forward to a world founded upon four essential human freedoms. The first is freedom of speech and expression...The second is freedom of every person to worship God in his own way...The third is freedom from want...The fourth is freedom from fear.'

President Franklin D. Roosevelt 1882-1945,
Address to Congress, 6 January 1941.

Acknowledgements

IN THE COURSE of researching this book I received a great deal of invaluable assistance from many people on both sides of the Atlantic. In England I would like to acknowledge the assistance of the late Rev. Norman Butcher, sometime Vicar of Barwick in Elmet and himself a keen local historian; the John Rylands University Library of Manchester; the Methodist Church Archives and History Committee, also of Manchester; and Mr. D. Colin Dews, Secretary of the Yorkshire branch of the Wesley Historical Society; the West Yorkshire Archive Service Leeds District Archives and Bradford District Archives; the Society of Genealogists, London; the British Library, London; the Borthwick Institute of Historical Research, York; the Yorkshire Archaeological Society, Leeds; and the United States Embassy in London. Dr. R. A. Morriss of the Department of Printed Books and Manuscripts at the National Maritime Museum, Greenwich, London answered my questions on sailing ships, Lucy Waitt, Picture Librarian at Greenwich provided the illustration of an emigrant vessel of the period and Miss Alison Boyle of the Thorner Historical Society gave me valuable information concerning the location of some of the older buildings in Thorner village. Mrs. E. Leeson helped with research at the Public Record Office in London, and Mrs. B. E. Sharp fulfilled a similar role at the Institute of Historical Research, York. In the United States my thanks are also due to the Church of Jesus Christ of Latter Day Saints, Salt Lake City, Utah; the National Library of Congress, Washington; the Illinois State Historical Society; the Illinois Department of Transportation, and Time Life Books Inc. of Alexandria, Virginia. I am also very grateful to Mr. Fred M. Jones of Urbana, Illinois and Mrs. Ralph Frye of the Great River Genealogical Society, Quincy, Illinois for so speedily and helpfully answering my plea for assistance in the quarterly Journal of the Illinois Historical Society.

The biggest debt of all however I owe to the Curry family, and to all the other descendants of John and Rebecca who have played their part in the search for freedom over the course of more than a hundred and seventy years. Without them it can truly be said that this book would never have been written.

Introduction

THIS IS THE STORY of a farming family from Yorkshire who with five of their children emigrated to the United States of America in 1831. Until I discovered the original account quite by chance in 1978, it had apparently lain undisturbed on a library shelf since its publication in 1848. However, although a fascinating account, in many respects it was disappointingly inadequate. Written anonymously, it began at the start of the journey and ended fourteen years later. But it gave no account of the circumstances that led to this dangerous venture, mentioned only one name - that of Rebecca, the wife and mother - and provided few details of the family background.

This book is an attempt to rectify these and other omissions. Using a variety of original and secondary sources, I have attempted to set the story in a national and local context, and having identified the people concerned, I have also tried to envisage the circumstances under which they lived their lives. Furthermore, the tracing of descendants of the family has allowed me to add an extra dimension by describing their own lives from the end of the original story up to the present day. Throughout my aim has been two-fold. To chronicle the considerable achievements of one very ordinary family, and to bring those achievements to a much wider audience.

Preface

THE COLONIZATION of the 'Wild West' is one of the best known events in history. However, the story is usually presented simply as a battle for territory and little is said of the social circumstances which during the nineteenth century, over the course of eighty years, caused an estimated ten and a half million people[1] - the equivalent of the entire population of England - to abandon their homes and face the horrors of an Atlantic crossing and the New World. Still less is said of the personal hardship endured by the families involved, many of whom were simple people, unlearned, impoverished, often in ill-health, frequently burdened with large families, and totally ignorant of the world beyond their own parish boundary, or of the despair which was responsible for such a major upheaval. Although the Acts of Enclosure have all too often been held to be solely responsible for emigration, they were in fact probably only one of the relevant factors. Others may have been the economic recession following upon the Napoleonic Wars, an increase in the population resulting from the return of soldiers from war, a fall in the death rate, inflationary food prices, industrial mechanisation and the administration of poor relief. Whatever the reason, the effect of such a desertion on the British working class population was dramatic.

As the pioneers left the shores of their home country for the other side of the world, they must have been well aware of at least some of the risks inherent in such a venture. Certainly they would have expected the consequences of their decision to be irrevocable for whatever misfortune befell them, and the possibilities were almost unlimited, the cost of travel and the distance involved made it highly unlikely that they would ever be able to return. Nor would keeping in touch have been an option open to them. Even supposing that they were literate, and most were not, communications between the new continent and the old were in their infancy. Although the packets carrying mail from Liverpool to the eastern seaboard of the United States averaged a run of only four to five weeks, it still took many months for a letter to reach its final destination. In effect therefore their departure signalled the permanent severance of family ties.

From the day they sold up in their native country early settlers experienced only fear. Fear of the unknown, fear of ill-health, above all fear of failure. They carried with them their entire life savings, often a meagre sum which had to be apportioned carefully and spent prudently. Most of their money had to be set aside for the purchase of land on arrival; the remainder barely covered the essential needs of the family. All forms of travel were hazardous and acutely uncomfortable. The early travellers were as astonished and apprehensive at the sight of a train or a ship as would be a modern tourist confronted by a space ship. Moreover many had no conception at all of the 'sea', and were consequently overwhelmed by the apparently limitless expanse of water which confronted them at the docks, and petrified at the prospect of having to cross it.

If they survived the rigours of shipboard life, no mean feat in itself, and elected not to remain in the American coastal towns, their journey was even further prolonged. As they continued to travel onward into the interior by waggon or on horseback, sometimes on foot or by way of the rivers, they encountered new hazards. In the early nineteenth century settlement was still principally confined to the eastern side of the country, but as the century progressed the frontier was pushed further and further back and the deeper the pioneers penetrated, the greater were their chances of meeting hostile Indian tribes. By that time their money was generally getting low, they had insufficient to eat and if any of them fell sick they either recovered spontaneously or died. No one will ever know for example how many children were buried in crude graves along the way, the victims of Indian hostility, disease, malnutrition, dirt or just plain negligence.

The burden on the women was particularly great; indeed it is tempting to suggest that it may have been they who suffered the most. Certainly the men were spared a great deal. The journey was quite arduous enough without pregnancy and its attendant perils and discomforts, giving birth in swaying, crowded, grimy waggons at the trailside or on the ground outside with little privacy and only the other women in the party for help. Nor had the men continually to contrive ways of caring for several small children and babies, difficult at all times but especially so within an hour or two of giving birth. The pioneer women would have had no time for exhaustion and certainly no notion at all of the 'vapours' so beloved of their more genteel contemporaries.

Some of the settlers, usually those going to join relatives or friends, had a destination in mind; others simply stopped in what seemed to them to be a suitable place. There were no maps available to them so they had no means of knowing where they were, and eventually it would be up to the settlers themselves to choose a name for their new home. If someone else had already earmarked the spot they had chosen, the newcomers would be driven off to seek another site. If however they were able to establish some kind of settlement, in due course they would probably be called upon to defend it themselves, either from the Indians or from other settlers.

Although many months may have passed since the day when the decision to emigrate had been taken, the fear they had felt then in no way abated when they eventually reached their destination. Until they had established their claim to a plot of land, built a home, acquired stock and fenced and cultivated at least a part of their holding, their new way of life was desperately precarious. The pioneers were of course no strangers to extreme hardship. Since infancy most had been familiar with oppression, poverty, hunger, sickness and bereavement, and adversity was consequently an essential constituent of their lives. That fact however should not be allowed to diminish the enormity of their achievement and while some floundered and sank under the pressure of it all, others were successful beyond their wildest dreams.

This story of one such family of pioneers and their experiences is not in itself unusual. The history of the United States contains many such accounts, some even more spectacular and dramatic. What is remarkable about this account is that it belongs essentially to a simple, working class woman possessed of great resolution and determination. Few of those early emigrant wives who contributed so much of value to the founding of a modern America left behind a record of their feelings and experiences. The rarity of such accounts renders them particularly valuable.

CHAPTER I

The Background to Emigration

AT THE END OF the eighteenth century England was ruled by the mad King, George III, governed by William Pitt the younger, and at war with France. She supported approximately six and a half million people of whom the vast majority earned their living on the land, while only two cities, London and Bristol, had a population larger than 50,000. Hitherto the production and processing of wool, centred in the north upon the cottage homes of the Pennine hills, had been the country's principal industry but now the period also marked the emergence of the manufacture of cotton.

The fact that the cotton industry expanded so rapidly was largely due to the beginning of the machine age. In 1765 James Hargreaves, an illiterate Lancashire labourer, stimulated by the sight of his daughter's upturned spinning wheel conceived the idea that several spindles could be rotated simultaneously in an upright position by one person. The invention of the Spinning Jenny, named after his daughter, created a minor revolution and in 1770 the patenting of Arkwright's Water Frame made it essential for the spinners to unite under one roof. It was this adoption of water power which was responsible for the proliferation of mills in the towns of northern England. In the thirty years up to 1790 importation of the raw material increased tenfold.

The last quarter of the eighteenth century also produced other inventions. In 1774 a Unitarian minister called Joseph Priestley from Birstall near Leeds found a way of isolating oxygen, while a few years later James Watt's steam engine and Henry Cort's puddling process laid the foundations of a golden era in the iron and steel industry. This was also the age of the canal, work on the Leeds and Liverpool beginning in 1770, and on the Grand Union in 1793. Destined to link London and Warwickshire the latter was followed by hundreds of miles of waterways crossing the countryside exposing hitherto inaccessible

1

areas to a cheap and efficient system of transport, and allowing goods to move around the country with comparative ease.

Without considerable improvement in the road system, however, economic expansion was still limited. In some places roads were maintained by Turnpike trusts, but mostly they were still the responsibility of the parishes through which they ran, and their condition was accordingly very variable. The turnpike road joining Preston and Wigan is said to have contained ruts four feet deep, while that between Chepstow and Newport was reputedly scattered with boulders as big as a horse. Accidents were frequent as carriages overturned and passengers thrown out; indeed for much of the year some of the roads were virtually impassable and wheels often had to be removed from the wagons so that they could be pulled along on their undercarriages like sledges.

To the discomfort of the passengers was added constant fear. Much of the countryside was covered with woods and heathland, ideal territory for the concealment of highwaymen and petty thugs so that every journey became a perilous undertaking fraught with apprehension. Some two hundred offences were punishable by death, and public executions were still commonplace occurrences, entertainments even, witnessed by large crowds to whom rotting corpses swinging from wayside gibbets weeks after the event were a familiar sight.

Philanthropic movements, while not as prolific as they were to become in the nineteenth century, were nevertheless very much in vogue. In 1777 John Howard, the High Sheriff of Bedfordshire, revolted by the degrading conditions which he had witnessed inside Bedford Gaol, began his battle to reform the English prison system, and in 1780 Robert Raikes was instrumental in organizing education on Sundays for poor children rather than actually founding the Sunday School movement as is sometimes supposed.[2] In 1790 a group of evangelical Christians calling themselves the Clapham sect campaigned on several social issues of the day. In 1807 one of their number, William Wilberforce, a Member of Parliament, was to see one of his ambitions realised when a Bill for the abolition of slavery in the West Indies was passed; regrettably he was denied the ultimate satisfaction of knowing that the Slavery Abolition Act was itself also passed one month after his death in 1833.

The age was also one of artistic distinction and exploration. While the Scottish Adam brothers, James and Robert, were engaged in the architectural embellishment of London, Samuel Taylor Coleridge and William Wordsworth were writing poetry at their homes in the

Quantock Hills, and in 1771 Tobias Smollett wrote his picaresque novel, Humphry Clinker. In 1775 a child called Jane was born in Hampshire to the Reverend George Austen and his wife, while four years later news came back to England that the explorer James Cook had been cruelly murdered by the natives of the Hawaiian Islands.

The importance of the church in every aspect of parish life cannot be over-estimated. In towns and villages all over the country churches were very tangible symbols of a religious presence at the heart of every-day life. Spiritually, administratively and socially the church repre-sented security and permanence, and provided a framework for the lives of those in the communities it served. In many parishes the gift of the living was held by the Lord of the Manor who took infinite pains to ensure that the views of the appointed incumbent harmonised with his own. Successful candidates were likely to be well-connected, a brother or nephew perhaps, even a younger son of some distant enno-bled family. Whatever their origins most were dedicated to hopes of a rapid climb up the ecclesiastical ladder of preferment, and originality of thought and independence of action were therefore seldom dis-played. When the holder of the benefice attended church on Sunday, at a time previously ordained by himself, he expected his wife, his chil-dren and his servants to be told what he was paying for them to hear. If they were not, then other arrangements could be made, and in an age over-endowed with clergymen both unbeneficed and impecunious, such changes were not difficult to effect.

While there is no doubt that many ministers worked long and hard in their parishes, becoming familiar and well loved figures, there is also ample evidence that others were considerably less than conscientious, intent only upon collecting their tithes and generally pursuing their own more worldly interests to the detriment of their flocks. Wining and dining lavishly around the best houses in the country, fishing, shooting and hunting several times a week, the sporting parson was tacitly accepted as an intrinsic part of rural England. Others less extro-vert devoted themselves to more scholarly pastimes, archaeology per-haps, or natural history; even the writing of a lengthy treatise on some obscure topic. In the tranquil seclusion of a country vicarage it was not difficult for the hobby to overtake the job.

Perhaps not surprisingly therefore, towards the end of the eigh-teenth century the working man became increasingly disillusioned with the Church of England. Run, so it seemed, by the establishment for the establishment, it appeared to offer little for those born into servitude with its attendant and incessant battle against poverty and starvation. Indeed, in some areas like the new mill towns growing up in lonely valleys, where the poor and illiterate desperately in need of direction formed the bulk of the population, there existed no parish at all. Lawlessness and drunkenness went hand in hand, and violence and despair controlled the lives of the masses. Only in an Anglican clergyman called John Wesley did thousands of them find their salvation.

From his pulpit in the Church of England, Wesley preached salvation by faith, 'the simple truth for simple folk',[3] but while his words struck a respondent chord in the hearts of many, the enthusiasm he generated earned him the disapproval of his superiors, and he was thus deprived both of a platform and a congregation. Undeterred, Wesley determined to take his message to a wider audience beginning in 1739 with a crowd of about three thousand in Bristol. It was the start of a new life as an itinerant preacher, the beginning of a 250,000 mile pilgrimage lasting fifty years. For those who went to hear him preach in homes and institutions, on village greens and moor tops, on the bleak mountains and in green valleys he brought new expectations. Into the disillusionment came the virtues of discipline, industry and temperance. Where there had once been incredulity, there was now faith. Where there had been despair there was hope. All over the land there occurred a surge of enthusiasm, a fresh belief in the power of Providence.

Although some of the Anglican clergy actively supported Wesley while contriving to remain loyal to the established church, others regarded him at best as a nuisance and at worst as a dangerous fanatic. Either way he made no great difference to the established order of parish life. A marriage was illegal unless it was performed in the Church of England, the only service permissible for the burial of the dead was from the Book of Common Prayer, and local government, magisterial office and the universities were open only to church communicants. Socially unacceptable as they were however, and despite arousing considerable suspicion particularly amongst the gentry, the Dissenters were on the whole tolerated provided they contributed towards the upkeep of their local church through the parish rates. Less tolerant however was the squire, hitherto an omnipotent force in rural life, who found this new surge of independence unwelcome. The autonomy he had always enjoyed had never previously been challenged; now he found it unthinkable that those he perceived as agitators should have the temerity to disturb the previously comparatively unruffled fabric of his existence. In the life of the village the holder of the lordship ranked second only to God; indeed, in the eyes of simple peasants seldom far removed from pagan superstition, and concerned more with the present than the promised land, he often appeared to be of premier importance, controlling as he did virtually every facet of their lives. As well as his authority over the church and its incumbent, a combination of birth and appointment rendered him responsible for everything and everyone in his community. London was far away and preoccupied with issues more important than the perceived trivialities of rural life. As a Justice of the Peace he governed the administrative and political life of the county. In sentencing the guilty, levying the rates, licensing inns and fairs and distributing relief to the parish poor along with a multitude of other tasks, the squire held sway over a miniature kingdom where his word was the only word of law.

In some parts of the country agricultural methods were beginning to progress after centuries of stagnation. This was the principal era of land enclosure when hedges first threaded their way across the old open field system to give us the more ordered landscape we see today. It was a scheme promoted by Arthur Young, Secretary of Agriculture, a farmer and agricultural writer who on his travels around the country was appalled to find archaic methods of food production, and who realised that without drastic land reorganisation the population would never be adequately fed. He believed that economic viability could never be achieved until the smallholdings and common land were gathered up and reapportioned into sizeable and well-cultivated estates. In the years between 1795 and 1812, 1,593 Acts of Enclosure were passed[4] and as soon as the land had been formed into large estates, the new owners invested considerable capital in improvement schemes.

From the point of view of the large estate owner the timing of the transfer of land from the poor to the rich could not have been more propitious. It coincided with the outbreak of war in 1793, with expanding markets and soaring prices, and with an enormous increase in the population which provided a plentiful supply of labour. Landowners were quick to take full advantage of the situation, ploughing their profits back into the land until more and more of it was brought under cultivation. Land in such good heart carried a high rental value, but the tenants did not object for as long as their crops were good and their stock healthy, they were well able to meet the financial demands made upon them. The letting of land was usually organised on a yearly basis although agreements could be rendered invalid at any time by either party at six months notice. Long leases were generally regarded with disfavour; it took time to assess the full potential of land and farmers disliked committing themselves to periods of seven, fourteen or even, in some cases, twenty one years.

Those most severely affected by the Enclosures were the cottagers. Before enforcement of the Act when they had tilled a small strip of parish land and enjoyed a commoner's right to graze cattle, pigs and chickens, grow their vegetables and gather fuel, they had been able to provide a means of subsistence for themselves and their families. Now they suffered arbitrary confiscation of this right, while compensation if any, proved to be totally inadequate. To compound further their hardship, the time-honoured rural crafts of spinning and weaving, in some areas traditionally theirs for centuries, were simultaneously withdrawn and concentrated in the new mills. Thus the cottagers were left with no choice but to surrender their independence and become hired hands, although that too was not without its difficulties. Land improvement schemes had created plenty of work, for example in hedging and ditching, but competition for it was great, and it was not long before wages were far outstripped by the rising cost of food and the population found itself facing starvation.

In 1795 an unsuccessful attempt was made to alleviate this suffering. A group of magistrates at Speenhamland in Berkshire met to decide that wages, instead of being raised, should be linked to the price of bread so that when the cost of a loaf was a shilling, every needy person and the members of his family should receive a subsidy from the poor rates. Thus as the price of bread rose so the dole rose with it, a measure which merely had the effect of allowing the wealthy employer to pay his men rock-bottom rates secure in the knowledge that the deficit would be made good by the parish, and at the same time placing an intolerable burden upon the less well-off, pauperising those men who were still fully employed. Moreover, the ruling made at Speenhamland only applied to those labourers with children; the more children, legitimate or illegitimate a man had, the more parish relief he received thereby rendering the childless labourer an undesirable prospect to any employer, an effect which critics of the scheme were eager to point out encouraged the poor to make imprudent marriages and procreate irresponsibly. Although such a pessimistic view may have been unwarranted, at least in part, there is little doubt that the Speenhamland policy proved to be disastrous and was to have a far-reaching effect on the early part of the nineteenth century.

CHAPTER II

Emigration

JOHN BURLAND WAS born at Thorner, a village six miles to the north-east of Leeds, in 1782. A linear village, the oldest property fronts the main road as it bypasses a ford and curves into a long straight between attractive stone houses, while the church of St. Peter, built of pale stone, stands at the north end of the main street. The second of eight children of Edward Burland, the village blacksmith and his wife, Mary, John was descended from a family which had farmed land at Thorner under the old open field system, but under the Enclosure Act of 1777 his grandfather, Stephen received one rood and eight perches of land on the southern fringe of the settlement.[5] It is probably he who in 1786 is described in the parish registers as a husbandman and who in 1769 served on the jury of the Rectory Manor.[6] At the time of John's birth the inhabitants of Thorner were very often inter-related, and Edward and Mary Burland relied on their relatives, friends and neighbours to provide most of the essentials of their lives. With a grocer, miller, wheelwright, cabinet maker, saddler, mason and shoemaker, all the main occupations essential to an isolated community were represented, and all save the Methodists among them might have been expected to meet up in The Fox or The Blue Boar of an evening.

Appropriately for a forge, the Burland's home, stood at the cross-roads in the centre of the village near Tarn House Farm. From there every Sunday the family walked along the main street to the parish church, filing into Pew 44 where they found themselves surrounded by friends and other families such as the Nettletons, Dalbys and Bickerdikes. While the Rev. Edward Carne read his weekly sermon, the younger children no doubt fidgeted alongside their parents, eager to return to the sunshine. In 1760 two houses in the village were licensed for the use of Methodists, one a dwelling house, the other a meeting house. William Burland was one of those to whom the licence was issued[7] and the Burland family, along with others, began to attend these meetings, no doubt thereby incurring the disapproval of their vicar. In 1764 when the Reverend John Fleming, Edward Carne's predecessor informed his Archbishop of these meetings, he tersely dismissed their existence with the comment 'How often they meet I do not know'.[8] Despite the fact that out of one hundred and twenty families in his parish, no fewer than thirty five of them were already Methodists, he apparently had not deemed it of sufficient importance to enquire further. In 1762 a building for public worship was licensed by the Methodists[9] near the crossroads on the opposite corner to the Burland's forge, but although Edward and Mary may have attended, their children would of necessity have been taken along the street to be baptised at St. Peter's. Indeed their seventh child, Edward, was also interred in the churchyard at the age of sixteen months. Infant mortality in those days was appallingly high and few people expected all of their children to reach maturity.

The four surviving sons and three daughters, seeking the sanctuary of the warm forge on bitter winter days, grew up in a secure and unchanging environment where the sense of community was strong. As the blacksmith Edward was something of a jack of all trades. In addition to the customary shoeing of the many horses in the district, he also manufactured and repaired household implements and tools and acted as the village veterinary surgeon and dentist, extracting the teeth of both animal and human victims. Often he worked in conjunction with other tradesmen, tyring wheels for the wheelwright or supplying the cabinet maker with metalwork fittings for coffins and furniture, and the regular flow of visitors to his forge must have ensured a steady supply of village gossip gleaned through the acrid fumes of burning hoof and against the background of the spasmodic tattoo of metal upon metal. The Burland children attended the village school in Thorner, situated by the church gates, where they learned the basic rudiments of reading, writing and arithmetic under the watchful eye of the Rev. Thomas Carr and his successor in 1798, William Midgley. Lessons over, the children were no doubt eager to spill out into the main street and make their way back to the forge.

Events of international or even national importance made little impact on village life. Louis XVI,. found guilty of treason, was executed in Paris in 1793, and a week later the Revolutionary Government of France declared war on Great Britain. Paradoxically towns and villages all over the country pounced on the situation as an excuse for celebrating to assure George III of their loyalty, and many addresses were delivered to that end. 'We heartily offer to your Majesty our firm support in the prosecution of the war with sincere assurances of firm attachment to your Majesty's person and family at this momentous juncture' reported the Leeds Intelligencer.[10] Bonfires were lit, sheep roasted, church bells pealed and everyone sang the National Anthem. Afterwards the villagers made their way home warmed by a combination of patriotism and alcohol, and armed with sufficient gossip to cast a little light relief into the boredom of the ensuing days.

While the Duke of York and his troops were being driven back by the French at Hondschoote that summer, agricultural England found itself sharply divided. As the rich grew ever richer, the position of the landless poor became increasingly parlous. Many of them were compelled to exchange the countryside for the towns, in the North of England often finding alternative employment in the very factories which had robbed them of their cottage industries. Shortly after the outbreak of this war John Burland left the family home in Thorner. It is not clear why he decided to do so for it was customary for the eldest son of a family to follow his father's trade. Perhaps he and his father had crossed swords - John was known to possess a quick temper - or maybe he merely had a desire to spread his wings away from family influence. There may however have been more fundamental reasons. The advent of the enclosure movement coupled with the post-war decline in agriculture had suddenly made the future appear much less stable. Moreover the emerging textile trades were having a marked effect on the local population providing a new focus for employment elsewhere.[11] Whatever the reason John went to Horsforth, a village some five miles north west of the city of Leeds, a move which may have been gained as a result of attending one of the local hiring fairs, or perhaps because of the offer of bed and board in return for his labour by a friend or relative. Such arrangements were not unusual, particularly in the north of England. Many farmers had a small army of retainers who worked as ploughboys, cowmen or stable lads, the only stipulation being that they were single men and willing to live in with the family. In such situations the sensible among them carefully saved as much of their wage as possible in the hope that one day they would have sufficient capital to lease a small property of their own.

John was a tall powerfully built youth with thick wavy hair, prominent cheek bones, a determined mouth and an infectious sense of humour. He came from a moral and deeply religious family whose belief in the teachings of John Wesley remained unshaken despite the temptations of the age in which he lived. Sobriety, economy and industry were the chief formative influences in the lives of all the Burland children, and John proved to be no exception. A strong-willed, principled and determined character, he might easily have chosen a quiet and submissive wife, but in fact he was fortunate enough to meet one of the few women who, despite being ten years his junior, would prove to be more than his match.

Rebecca Burton was born on the 18th May, 1793, four months after the declaration of war between France and England, the third daughter of John and Mary Burton at Durcar, or Dirtcar as it was then known, on the south side of Leeds. Like her seven siblings Rebecca was baptised at the parish church of Sandal Magna two miles away on the outskirts of Wakefield where her father, an agricultural labourer, was much respected. Becca, as she was known at home, grew into a slender girl of medium height who suffered severely from asthma. Honest, hard-working and sensible she was also literate, unusual in a girl of her social status, part of her education having been gained at a local day school for which John Burton paid the then princely sum of five shillings per annum. It is difficult to understand how an agricultural labourer was able to afford such a sum, particularly when there were seven other children to consider. Even more incomprehensible is the fact that despite this expenditure, it was not until Rebecca attended a Wesleyan Sunday school at nearby Horbury that she learned to read fluently. During the winter months the young Rebecca also helped her mother with the large family and in summer spent much of her time in the lanes and on the common land around her home where she tended three or four cows. Each morning as soon as the cattle had been milked, Rebecca drove them to their grazing, a basket on her arm containing food and knitting and a book of Charles Wesley's hymns which she sang while manufacturing socks and stockings for the family. Literate or not however, a life in service was the lot of almost all girls of her background, and at the age of thirteen Rebecca found herself bound for Wakefield on a carriers cart for the first stage of the twenty mile journey to Horsforth. Never previously absent from home, or separated from her family, she must have presented a forlorn figure as she waved goodbye to her parents, siblings and the familiar surroundings of her home village.

Rebecca's destination can perhaps be explained by the fact that much of Horsforth was then owned by Walter Spencer Stanhope, an absentee landlord whose chief residence was at Cannon Hall, Cawthorne, only six miles from Durcar. He is known to have been acquainted with the Rev. Henry Zouch during the latters' incumbency as Rector of Sandal at a time when the rector was also a trustee of the Lady Mary Bolles Charity. This provided funds for '...binding poor children of the Parish of Sandall [sic] yearly apprentices,[12] and members of the Burton family may have received help from this charity in the past. Great care was usually taken in such circumstances to ensure that beneficiaries were placed in employment well outside their own parish to avoid any possibility of their becoming a burden on the poor rates. Although Henry Zouch had ceased to be Rector of Sandal by the time Rebecca left home, his successor as rector and trustee of the charity, the Rev. William Brown, may well have continued this useful link with Horsforth.

It is quite likely that Rebecca went to work in the house of a local farmer, and it is even possible that she and John worked for the same man, perhaps Thomas Rider, a smallholder on the Stanhope estate and one of the witnesses at their subsequent wedding. However the records of the poor are invariably inadequate, and there is little information of the time John and Rebecca spent in Horsforth. Whatever the circumstances of their meeting we know no more of them until the 2nd December, 1811, ten months after the proclamation of George IV as Regent, when the couple were married at St. Oswald's Church, Guiseley, three miles from Horsforth. Early nineteenth century Guiseley consisted of a huddle of dour stone cottages sprawling across the southern slope of a high ridge of land with a church perched well above the main street alongside an Elizabethan rectory. For centuries it had been attended by people from the surrounding villages for baptism, marriage and burial, amongst them the ancestors of Henry Wadsworth Longfellow who lay beneath a confusion of ancient, lichened gravestones. Just a year after John and Rebecca's wedding, on the 29th December, 1812 the Rev. Patrick Bronte and Miss Maria Branwell celebrated their own marriage here, little realising then that one day they would become known throughout the world as the parents of the famous novelist sisters, Charlotte, Emily and Anne. John and Rebecca signed the marriage register in front of the Rev. Thomas Hamilton and their two witnesses, emerging from the church to greet a small group of friends and well-wishers who had congregated in the wintry sunshine, before travelling back to Horsforth by waggon.

Here in the gritstone country in the foothills of the Pennines, the land was shallow and poor, more suited to sheep than crops, and accordingly there had been little haste to enclose it. However with the aid of a strip of land in the common fields and the right to graze his cattle on the waste land, John was able to eke out some kind of existence for the two of them. In the early summer of 1813, while Wellington was advancing across Spain towards the French at Vitoria,

Rebecca gave birth to their first child, a delicate boy baptised Edward after John's father and two years later, on the 26th February, 1815, the day on which Napoleon escaped from captivity on the Island of Elba, the couple baptised their second infant, Mary. Four months later twenty three years of war at last came to an end.

Almost immediately England began to suffer for her defeat of Napoleon. The soldiers returned, and like soldiers before and since they found a country enormously in debt, heavy taxation, unemployment and widespread discontent. As the war had progressed, prices had continued to rise. Poor seasons, the state of the currency, the price of transport, the rise in population and blockaded ports, all no doubt played a substantial part in the recession. For a long time agriculturalists had been riding high. Now they found themselves experiencing their worst ever depression. Even before the end of the war the price of corn had slumped; the cessation of hostilities merely accelerating that decline. Thus the landowners whose capital had been sunk in land enabling them to enjoy the high profits of the war years, hastily appealed for legislation in order to protect themselves against the importation into the re-opened ports of cheap corn from the Continent. In March of 1815 this was granted and until such time as home-produced corn reached 85 shillings a quarter (512 lbs.) foreign corn was not permitted to enter the country.[13] Such measures however did not result in the economic stability the landlords had anticipated. The landowners' economy was also dependent upon the ability of their tenants to pay high war-time rents, but in a depressed market the situation of the tenants became increasingly desperate. Faced with demands for tithe, an iniquitous practice which farmers had endured since the tenth century and with tradesmen's bills, taxes and rent, they had little choice but to relinquish their leases and sell their stock for whatever price they were offered in order to try to settle their debts. Others meanwhile who had no intention of settling anything, vanished overnight with whatever money and possessions they were able to salvage.

As agriculture was the backbone of village life, the burden on the Poor Law accordingly became immense. Tradesmen, innkeepers and shopkeepers suffered as acutely as the farmers themselves, and perhaps for this reason Edward now decided to retire from the forge in Thorner leaving Stephen to follow his brother to Horsforth where he was to work the forge with his youngest sons, John and Thomas. 1816 was a particularly bad year. Heavy summer rains brought flooding, a disastrous potato crop and a ferocious winter which destroyed entire flocks of sheep. More and more destitute and desperate farmers abandoned agriculture altogether but John, who had prudently amassed a little capital, elected to remain in farming. In 1817 he and Rebecca took a fourteen year lease on a small farm at Barwick in Elmet,[14] not far from Thorner, a mile from the road which runs between Leeds and Tadcaster, where the arable lands of East Yorkshire meet the dairylands of the west.

CHAPTER III

Pastures New

JOHN AND REBECCA'S choice of Barwick may have had something to do with family connections for the parish registers of Barwick reveal numerous Burland entries. It is indeed probable that earlier Burlands had moved there from Aberford, a couple of miles away, for their family name first appears in those registers in the early sixteenth century.

The village of Barwick, believed to derive its name from "berewic", a barley growing place,[15] has its roots firmly set in pre-Christian times. A huge maypole, symbol of pagan fertility rites stands in the centre of the village, while Hall Tower Hill is reputedly the site of the palace of Edwin, first Christian king of Northumbria. As at Thorner, the old farmsteads cling to the side of the road which winds between cottages, an inn, the rectory and the stone church of All Saints. When John and Rebecca lived in the village, life was little changed from medieval times. Christmas and Candlemas, Shrove Tuesday and Easter, Mayday and Ascension Day, the annual feast, the harvest supper and rent day were all important annual milestones often providing welcome diversions in lives that were otherwise hard and bleak.

On the land as well as in the house the most primitive methods were still employed. Seed was sown broadcast, farmsteads were cold, draughty and damp and devoid of drainage, water had to be fetched from the village pump several hundred yards away, and clothing was mostly homespun. Meals were wholesome but simple. There was no roasting, meat and vegetables being boiled in a pot suspended from a reckon and crane over the fire. Bread was baked in a side oven, and a griddle was used for the baking of havercake. Rebecca also made her own butter, a prolonged and laborious task. Poured into large vats the milk was set aside in order to allow the cream to rise and in cold weather this had to be churned for many hours, a tedious chore with which the children were all expected to help. Finally when the butter 'came',

Rebecca worked it in the hand expelling the buttermilk before patting it into shape with wooden moulds. Skimmed milk was fed to the pig which was usually bought during the summer so that it could be fattened up in time for Christmas. A pig killing was an important event in the calendar. Every part of the animal was a valuable source of food and the thrifty Rebecca wasted nothing. As soon as the dead pig had been scalded enabling the men to remove the bristles, it was jointed to produce hams, shoulders, spare ribs and belly. The heart, liver and tongue were equally valuable as were any spare bits of meat which were collected carefully. Chopped finely, mixed with sage and rolled into balls, they made tasty sausages. Even the pig's blood was preserved in buckets so that black puddings, a traditional Yorkshire savoury delicacy, could be made. The smoky atmosphere inside the cottages also necessitated the frequent cleaning of stone flagged floors and tabbed rugs, while washday precipitated such an upheaval that it was only undertaken once every five weeks.

To add to this domestic toil were the births of an apparently interminable succession of children. Families of ten or fifteen were commonplace in the village, several more babies being on the way at any one time, and if their mothers needed a reminder of their tenuous hold on life, the passing bell of All Saints frequently tolled for infant victims of diseases we would today regard as no more than trivial inconveniences. At the beginning of the nineteenth century the average life expectancy was about thirty seven years.[16] Women relied on each other for considerable support in their day to day life in the home just as the men depended on each others help in the fields. It was a closely-knit community where they dropped in and out of each others houses offering help and seeking advice, borrowing and lending, sharing innumerable worries and supervising their own and everyone elses' children. Above all it was a world where each person had his or her own place and kept to it, and where the shadow of the workhouse loomed large.

It soon became apparent that John and Rebecca's move had been unwise. Lucky farmers had their rents based on pre-war prices, but John was not so fortunate. His holding was too small and his rent too high and during the years he and Rebecca were at Barwick they were helped through only as a result of their thrift and industry. While there appeared to be little prospect of any improvement in their financial circumstances, their family was increasing rapidly. Jane was born in 1817, Anne in 1819 and John in 1821, but 1822 brought sorrow. On the 1st March, Anne died suddenly, followed five days later by her sister Jane, both victims of scarlet fever. They were buried together in the churchyard at Barwick, but although Rebecca no doubt often went to their graveside there was little time to mourn. The farm claimed all the couples' attention and Rebecca had somehow to fit into the daylight hours all of the chores from which there was never any escape. Moreover there were still three children to be cared for, and within weeks Rebecca knew that she was pregnant once again. In the spring of 1823, Hannah was born and baptised at the church where her sisters had so recently been buried. Stephen died within three months of his birth in 1825, and his sisters Charlotte and Sarah were born in 1826 and 1828 respectively. In February 1830 two more children, Harriet and Maria, who may have been twins, died in infancy.

In due course the Burland children attended the village school, a stone building set in one corner of the churchyard which also served as their playground where they fought, chased and laughed over the graves of their sisters and brother. They were especially fortunate in their educational opportunities. Few parents in those days recognised the need for an education and even fewer could afford to provide it. Barwick School was presided over by the parish clerk, a strict and learned Scot called John Irvine who received £23 a year to rule his pupils with an iron hand. During his time in the village his forthright manner earned him several enemies among the parents, but John and Rebecca found themselves in sympathy with his high principles, and for the price of a penny a week per child, welcomed his disciplined influence. Edward in particular flourished under the guidance of the man who proved to be a life-long source of inspiration.

Out of school the young Burlands ran wild with all the other village children. They knew all the narrow twisting lanes and paths, the shaded woods which eased into spring with celandines and wood anemones before the early summer days brought forth a haze of bluebells. By the Cock Beck they gathered primroses and violets and caught minnows in the deep, dark pools by the bridge. They probed deep into hedgerows for nests and eggs, lazed in the grass to blow dandelion clocks and manufacture daisy chains, fed hungrily on the blackberries which grew in every hedge, and slaked their thirst with ice-cold water from the Town Well. At night they dared each other to visit Asses Bridge where it was said they would see a saucer-eyed padfoot with clanking chains, while in the appropriate seasons they spun tops or played with marbles at the foot of the village cross, a place where the old men smoked their pipes and talked away the hours, and women paused briefly to grumble that meat was now three and a half pence per pound and a stone of oatmeal cost two shillings and twopence.

Much of the village entertainment was based on ancient custom. It was near the cross that the children, warmed by leaping flames and chunks of havercake soaked in mugs of hot broth, held their annual bonfire on November 5th, until 1835 an event subsidised in Barwick by the church to the tune of between one shilling and two shillings and sixpence for gunpowder and coal. Another highlight was the May Day celebration when Barwick's ninety foot maypole was lowered for decoration with flower garlands prior to an official rearing ceremony. One memorable year the much prized pole was stolen by youths from a nearby village and Barwick's passions were roused. Old men and women, outraged by the theft, urged the young to action, and fifteen year old Edward joined the inter-village conflict brandishing a cudgel. Honour was only restored when the men returned to Barwick triumphantly bearing the pole, and the Whitsuntide festivities to promote crop and animal fertility could go ahead.

The village had many characters all of whom were known to the children. As well as old Maggie, widely regarded as a witch and believed to be blessed with second sight, there was William Dawson, steward and colliery agent to the Gascoigne family from Parlington Hall at Aberford, who was a well-known itinerant Wesleyan Methodist preacher, addressing his following with evangelistic fervour in the Barwick Chapel which was tucked discreetly into a corner of the village where it was hoped it would give rise to the minimum of offence. From 1758 until its opening in 1804, Barwick's Methodists had met in the house of another Burland, Richard, a weaver and formerly a York merchant, who was considered a public nuisance by those attending the village church. In 1792 there were said to be fourteen members led by a farmer Peter Newby and his wife Ann, daughter of Richard Burland and his wife, Dorothy.[17] Another cast in the same mould as William Dawson was Thomas Stoner, the miller and an exceedingly pious itinerant minister. Known as "old Tommy" and prominent in village life, his personal motto embodied all that Methodism stood for, 'diligent in business, fervent in spirit, serving the Lord'.[18] Leaving his home at the mill early every morning, he attended the 7.00 a.m. prayer meeting without fail winter and summer alike. Each Sunday, as well as two prayer meetings, he also attended worship twice, and taught morning and evening Sunday School. There was also the Barwick blacksmith, a mettlesome man whom the children often baited beyond endurance, his roars of fury sending them scurrying to safety, and the shoemaker, Matthew Allatt, a gentle kindly man who earned the undying affection of young Edward by rescuing him from the torments of two of the village bullies. Indeed Allatt's shop was to Barwick what the Burland forge had been to Thorner, a meeting place where the events of the village as well as those of the wider world were discussed endlessly. Meanwhile, at the Rectory, the Rev. William Hiley Bathurst, who baptised five of the Burland children, divided his time between maintaining a strict watch on the spiritual welfare of the villagers, collecting his dues in lieu of tithe and writing hymns.

Rebecca, who first became a Wesleyan Methodist as a result of a dream following a disastrous game of cards shortly after her marriage, was a frequent attender at the tiny chapel and drew strength from her Bible, for John was apparently not always an easy husband. His honesty, industry and integrity appear never to have been in doubt, and he was capable of showing his wife and children great affection but he seems also on occasion to have been possessed of a quick temper. The two of them were however also in need of guidance in other respects. In the 1820's the price of corn, forever fluctuating, started to rise again while a cow, which would have fetched fifteen pounds in 1813, was now worth only three. Consequently a wave of panic swept throughout the countryside. Like thousands of other small farmers who were proud and independent, and accustomed to working hard for little financial reward, John was sickened by his plight and the system which permitted it. He was weary of the constant struggle to pay his bills and feed his family, and depressed by the poverty and despair he saw in the village. Many of his friends and neighbours had already left for nearby towns which were now beginning to expand rapidly, but he found the prospect unattractive preferring instead to consider what he was increasingly coming to regard as the only remaining alternative.

For some time the economic problems and political unrest in England had spurred many families to seek their future abroad. Every week thousands of men, women and children left the country, destined in particular for America to which they were enticed by the prospect of purchasing their own rich, virgin soil. The literate, eager to write home bragging of their successes, painted a glowing and often highly exaggerated picture of the virtues of their new country, accounts which frequently lost nothing in the telling. Meanwhile those who had been less successful, perhaps not unnaturally maintained a discreet silence, a fact which did nothing to help present a truly accurate picture of the reality of the situation.

The possibilities offered by emigration had for some time appealed strongly to John. Moreover he was just the type to benefit from them, a good farmer, fit, physically strong, hard-working and with a little money. Too cautious by nature to act on impulse however, he renewed links with old friends from childhood days in an effort to discover the facts for himself. The Bickerdikes, another staunch Methodist family who lived at Carr Farm at Thorner, a mile or so across the fields from the centre of that village, had two sons several years John's junior. Some years previously the older, George, had given up his job as an ostler in Bradford, emigrating to Flint township, Pike County in the state of Illinois, and before long letters containing accounts of his success there had been received at home by his younger brother, John.

Rebecca to say the least was frightened and dismayed by this fresh turn of events. Neither she nor John had ever been more than thirty miles from home. Emigration would mean that they would have to leave virtually everything behind for a strange land of which they knew nothing. They were only vaguely aware of the ocean to be crossed, the discomforts to be endured and the hazards they would encounter. They did not know how much it would cost nor how long it would take, where they would live or even how they would manage to secure some land when they arrived, providing of course that they did arrive which on the face of it seemed to be highly unlikely. Their family had recently increased to seven with the birth of William in May, and the decision once taken would be final. For better or worse they would be committed. They would have to leave their roots, their friends and their relatives for ever. Not unnaturally Rebecca found herself awaiting her husband's return with more apprehension than eagerness.

John rode home from Barwick through fields bathed by the evening sun, his mind full of uncertainty and fear. Before him there lay the possibility, hitherto unconsidered, of owning his own unfettered fertile land, the prospect of a good life and a heritage for his children and their children. Like Rebecca he was far from blind to the many risks. He recognised that the danger to all of them was enormous, yet the rewards if they were fortunate enough to be able to take advantage of them could be great. With so much to be gained and the knowledge that others before him had succeeded, how could he turn aside such an opportunity? Their lease was due to expire in two months and the final decision could not be delayed. Soon the harvest would be in for yet another year and celebrated in the village church, the stubble peeling away from the plough ready to perpetuate the old inadequate way of life. The corn and oats through which he rode rippled in the light evening breeze. In the woods a pigeon cooed and overhead a skein of geese trailed out against the evening sky. It would be hard to leave all this behind, but in his heart he knew that it was what they must do.

He felt as if he had been channelled into a narrow tunnel with no alternative but to forge ahead in the hope of finding light at the end. This was probably the only opportunity they would ever have to make something of themselves, to build for the future rather than existing only for the present.

Rebecca must have received his news with resignation but knowing where her duty lay she was ready to set aside her own fears and feelings, and prepare for what to her would be the greatest sacrifice, separation from her two oldest children. Edward now eighteen had been a sickly child since infancy, and was quite unfitted for work on the land. Fortunately he was also a bright boy who had learned much from John Irvine, and had become an under-teacher at a nearby school in West Garforth where he was settled and happy. Mary, his sixteen year old sister was also away, in service with a good family. No matter what the cost to themselves she and John were unanimous in their agreement that the futures of these two children must not be jeopardised. For their own good Edward and Mary must stay behind in England. Soon they would marry and have families of their own. In the meantime they had several relatives who would keep an eye on them and to whom they would be able to turn in a crisis. As for the dangers to the remainder of her family, Rebecca did as she had always done and put her trust in God.

CHAPTER IV

Departures

THE DECISION TAKEN, John lost no time in going ahead with his plans. The lease of their farm expired, the stock was dispersed and arrangements made for the journey to Illinois. Deciding which of their possessions to take proved a fairly simple task for they owned so little. Eventually they settled on two straw-filled mattresses, some blankets, a little food, cooking utensils, a few farm implements and only one piece of furniture, Rebecca's rocking chair from which she steadfastly refused to be separated. What little remained they disposed of to relatives and neighbours. As the days wore on into late summer they felt increasingly as if they were living in limbo. With their arrangements complete, the harvest in for the last time and their stock gone, they spent time visiting relatives; several of John's brothers and sisters lived in the vicinity and Rebecca's brothers still farmed in Sandal. However, although they found the farewells a melancholy affair, the children became increasingly exhilarated by the impending move and were impatient to be away to start their new life.

The last week of August 1831 brought the waggon which was to take them to Manchester on the first leg of their journey. In the farmyard John loaded up their belongings while Rebecca, accompanied by Edward and Mary, looked on sadly. At that moment, despite all the difficulties, she would have given much to have abandoned everything to remain in their home. The younger children climbed eagerly onto the top of the load, squabbling as they sought out the most comfortable places to sit, while Rebecca, carrying baby William wrapped tightly in a shawl, braced herself for the moment of separation from her two eldest children. Taking her gently by the arm, John helped her onto the waggon and gruffly give the order to move off. Rebecca watched her son and daughter standing together in the road, Edward's arm wrapped protectively around the shoulders of his sister. As the waggon rumbled slowly along Barwick's main street in the direction of Leeds, Rebecca scarcely noticed as their friends and neighbours stood in the lane to wave farewell.

Although the waggon was a cumbersome, lumbering and acutely uncomfortable means of transport, its canvas roof did at least provide shelter, and it also allowed the emigrants to take a larger amount of luggage. Many who were unable to afford the relative luxury of transport had no option but to walk the whole way to the docks, leading their children and carrying only what luggage they could manage between them. Occasionally they contrived to beg lifts on passing farm waggons but the trek still took many days, and nights had to be passed at the side of lanes, in ditches and in hedgerows. A hay-filled barn was a luxury indeed. No inn, not even a rough wayside tavern, wanted any truck with vagrants for that was what the travellers appeared to be.

The route taken by the family followed the turnpike road from Leeds to Manchester through the West Riding villages of Dewsbury, Huddersfield, Marsden and Delph, and the Lancashire town of Oldham. It crossed some of the most desolate territory in England where in winter the searing winds of the moortops blanched the skin, and only the more hardy residents were able to endure the bitter, penetrating cold. Already, although only the end of August, the landscape was very different from that which they had left behind. This was harsher, far less hospitable country, veined by old packhorse trails which slithered erratically over the stony sheep-grazed hillsides to terminate in turbulent grey skies, while black drystone walls bounded irregular patches of scrubland bespattered with shrivelled hawthorn trees.

In the low stone cottages which dotted these steep hills, untold generations had lived out their lives, processing the fleeces of their sheep, eating, working and sleeping in an atmosphere thick with the pungent stench of greasy wool. This state of affairs had continued until the men who called themselves manufacturers had taken the industry down into the new mills in the wooded valleys, the 'sweat shops', which had prompted men such as Richard Oastler to fight for the improvement of working conditions. In these buildings children as young as five years of age were often savagely beaten while working a thirteen hour day six days a week, and as a result of poor nutrition and the constant stooping necessary to crawl under the spinning frames, many of the little pieceners as they were known in the trade because they pieced together the ends of the spun yarn, had acquired hideous deformities of their growing bones. As the waggon creaked and swayed its way into Lancashire, tossing the family around like helpless puppets, it passed some of these children at the side of the road, miserable waifs inadequately clad who gazed suspiciously from pinched and prematurely aged faces.

Progress was slow and the day seemed interminable especially for five year old Charlotte and three year old Sarah propped uncomfortably between the rocking chair and the tools. Fortunately they soon fell into a deep sleep, apparently undisturbed by the exclamations and chatter of young John and Hannah for whom the novelty of the occasion had not yet worn thin. Their parents meanwhile, stiff with cold and inactivity, welcomed the opportunity to climb down and walk, leaving the horses to ascend the steep hills, straining in the shafts.

It was early evening before they arrived in the centre of Manchester, hungry, cold and exhausted. The children were irritable and tearful, and little William, gnawing hungrily at his fists, writhed fretfully in his mother's arms. While John led the way in search of overnight accommodation at a cheap tavern, the children meekly followed, leaving Rebecca lagging behind to take in her surroundings. The appearance of Manchester did little to uplift her jaded spirits. Far bigger than she could ever have imagined she saw a towering jungle of smoke-blackened buildings conceived by the booming cotton trade, a noisy, crude and frightening town, smelling nauseatingly of decay and dyehouses. Groups of drunken, brutish men loafed at street corners shouting bawdy songs or fighting like animals in the rubbish-strewn alleys, tiny children crawled barefoot in the filthy gutters scavenging for scraps of food, while prostitutes splashed the grey streets with their cheap gaudiness. Rebecca marvelled that life in Barwick could ever have been considered unsatisfactory. In the space of only twelve hours she found herself in a totally alien environment of hitherto unimagined squalor where every vice seemed to prevail, and the Christian virtues she so cherished appeared to be unknown. This was her first real insight into the need for men like William Dawson who preached the Gospel in the chapel at home, and were passionate advocates of their faith, striving vigorously to transmit to those they perceived as belonging to the lower strata of society, a belief in themselves, the necessity for self-discipline and a strong moral code.

To her immense and undisguised relief it was not long before Rebecca found herself and her family safely settled in a tavern able to provide them with accommodation for one night. Although both the food and the accommodation were indifferent in quality, their first day on the road had left them all too exhausted to care, and even the strangeness of their surroundings and the noise from the street below failed to prevent them from sleeping. Next morning they rose early, refreshed and ready to travel on to Liverpool by the new railway which had now been operating between the two cities for a year.

Because Manchester had become the cotton empire of England, and Liverpool was ideally positioned for the importation of the raw material from the southern United States, hard-headed Manchester businessmen had been quick to see a need for speedy transportation between port and mill, essential for the expansion of their trade. Therefore George Stephenson, together with his son Robert, had been made responsible for constructing a rail link, a project which had proved to be both lengthy and extremely taxing. Despite a disastrous opening ceremony in 1830 when the local Member of Parliament and former Secretary of War for the Colonies, William Huskisson fell into the path of Stephenson's "Rocket" and subsequently died from the injuries he sustained,[19] the line had proved to be a tremendous asset. Besides opening up trade, hundreds of people, many from far afield, flocked to sample the new experience and indeed in society circles, considerable prestige was to be gained from having undertaken the journey.

The Burland family boarded the train at Manchester's Liverpool Road Station. The so-called carriages were in fact no more than open-topped trucks, completely devoid of seats, in which the passengers were so herded together that they stood shoulder to shoulder swaying in a mass, half-choked with smoke and spattered with soot and burning cinders. Despite their discomfort however John and Rebecca were awestruck by the experience of moving at speed across country and the miracle of engineering which had provided tunnels, bridges and viaducts to combat the natural contours of the land. On either side of the line there were new things to see, and ten year old John became so excited that he spent most of the journey in imminent danger of falling over the side onto the tracks. When the train rumbled across the impressive seventy foot high Sankey Viaduct, John senior became almost as excited as his son while Rebecca, finding the drop on either side quite terrifying, closed her eyes tightly.

In sharp contrast to their primitive journey of the day before, the train proved surprisingly fast and stable, and in only a little over an hour they were crawling through the deep sandstone cutting of Olive Mount and into the labyrinth of tunnels beneath the city of Liverpool and Crown Street station. Once again Rebecca remained behind with the children while John went in search of suitable lodgings. When he eventually returned it was to report that he had been successful in securing one room in a dingy street at a cost of two shillings a day. Rebecca regarded this as being nothing less than extortion, an opinion she saw no reason to revise when she was able to inspect the premises for herself. A solitary window looked directly onto a smoky wall, the room itself was dirty and bug-infested, and the total absence of any cooking facilities meant that for the duration of their stay they would be restricted to a dry diet.

Such squalid surroundings made it imperative for John to arrange their passage without delay. Every tide brought into port ships from America carrying cotton, timber and tobacco, their captains dependent on a lucrative return cargo of emigrants collected for them by the ship's brokers. Captain and emigrant had no direct contact. Instead the broker acted as a go-between receiving either a commission from the shipping company for every berth sold, or chartering a ship on his own and cramming it with as many passengers as he could muster, regardless of safety factors. Perhaps George Bickerdike had alerted John to the need for caution in this respect for when later that first day he booked the berths for his family, he was careful to put down only a deposit. This was a wise move. It was not uncommon for emigrants to part with the whole of their fare, at that time about nine pounds ten shillings, only to find themselves stranded when the broker absconded.

While they waited for the day on which their ship was to set sail, time once more hung heavily on their hands. As always Rebecca did her best to hold everyone together but it was not easy in such miserable and overcrowded accommodation. The children were fractious from a combination of tiredness, unaccustomed confinement and a strong sense of anti-climax, and ever since he had arrived in Liverpool, John himself had become increasingly despondent and withdrawn. During the journey from Barwick the constantly changing landscape and new experiences had given him little time for reflection, but now the waiting provided ample opportunity for his doubts to surge to the surface. He was also deeply saddened by the loss of Edward and Mary, a separation which had cut deeper than he had imagined and felt that he had deserted his children at a crucial period in their lives, that he and Rebecca should have remained in England until their future was more secure. As the days passed Rebecca was aware of his distress and of the sleepless nights and the days spent silently brooding, but she shared his concerns too closely to be able to offer any real comfort. On their sixth day in Liverpool, the day on which they were due to embark, with their last minute preparations almost complete, John abruptly announced that their plans would have to be abandoned. The responsibility was more than he felt able to undertake, the risks were too great. No matter how bleak their prospects he felt there was no alternative but to cancel the berths and make arrangements for an immediate return to Barwick. The suddenness and the apparent finality of this decision threw Rebecca into a state of utter confusion. Emigration had certainly never been her choice, and there was nothing in the world she would rather do than return to Edward and Mary, her old home and their friends. On the other hand she knew that it would never be enough for John. Although initially he would be delighted to be reunited with his children, the circumstances which had forced them to sell up in the first place were unchanged. If they were now to return to Barwick she felt convinced that he would always regret the fact that if he had not at the last lacked courage, everything might have been so very different. Despite her convictions however she was unwilling to speak out. Obedience to the wishes of her husband ensured that she kept her own counsel, tacitly agreeing to do whatever he thought best.

Their change of plan however produced no corresponding rise in John's spirits. Once they had retrieved their luggage from the docks and were back in the damp and smelly room, he became even more downcast and morose than before, showing none of the relief which might have been expected in the circumstances. Eventually Rebecca felt that she could keep silent no longer, pointing out that for many months they had worked and schemed towards a better life and that she was convinced their decision to emigrate was the right one. Edward and Mary were now quite capable of leading independent lives, but the younger children still needed to be provided for. Moreover, a return to Barwick meant a return to no land, no home, few possessions and little money. They must do as they had done in the past and go forward into the future. Her selflessness had the desired effect. Encouraged that the responsibility was no longer his alone, John, with renewed confidence arranged for their luggage to be restored to the ship while Rebecca, fully resigned to a future she dreaded but had nevertheless wholeheartedly embraced, did some last minute shopping for food and cooking utensils. Oatmeal, flour, bacon, biscuits, tea and coffee would she calculated be sufficient to feed them during the voyage, especially as they would be supplemented by rations they would be able to obtain on board. At sunset on Friday, the 2nd September, 1831, the 410 ton barque "Home," the Burland family aboard, slid quietly out from the port of Liverpool bound for New Orleans[20] and a new life.

CHAPTER V

The Voyage

IT HAD BEEN George Bickerdike's idea that they should approach their destination via New Orleans and the Mississippi River. The Mississippi and the Ohio Rivers were the main routes for migrants into the interior of the country[21] and although New Orleans was the most distant port in America, the route had the advantage of offering easy access to the centre of the country. In contrast disembarkation at the more usual ports of entry, New York, Boston, Baltimore and Philadelphia would have entailed a great deal of rugged land travel. These eastern seaboard towns contained a high percentage of emigrants whose original intention had been to settle far inland but who, because of their poverty, or because they were daunted by the prospect of crossing the Appalachian mountain range, some 1200 miles in length, had instead remained in the coastal cities.

In the 1830's emigration was becoming big business. In 1832 alone an estimated 103,000 people emigrated from the United Kingdom, mostly for the United States of America,[22] a total nearly three times greater than that recorded thirteen years earlier. Certainly Rebecca, leaning over the rail of the "Home" as it left Liverpool, was amazed at the number of ships in port and the towering forest of masts stretching far away into the distance. The evening breeze was favourable, and while the ship made rapid progress she remained on deck alone with her thoughts, gazing wistfully at vessels going into port. Only when the last faint shadow of land had completely faded from view did she turn away, wrapping herself more tightly in her shawl and resolutely going below, suddenly in urgent need of occupation.

In some respects the Burlands were probably more fortunate than most other emigrants for the "Home" seems to have been a reasonably well-run ship with a captain unusually concerned for the welfare of his steerage passengers. In 1823 and 1825 Passenger Acts were drawn up to obviate over-crowding on emigrant ships, the law requiring that a large white letter 'P' should be prominently displayed on every vessel with a ratio of more than one passenger to every five tons.[23] A later Act decreed that no ship was allowed to sail from Great Britain to any place outside Europe carrying more than three persons to every five tons.[24] Although theoretically these ships were then liable for inspection by Government officers on the high seas, such regulations, as with others so readily conceived by Parliament, were usually impossible to implement. Ships continued to be grossly overloaded and steerage passengers in particular were accommodated in conditions more suited to the transportation of cattle.

Embarkation, usually delayed until the moment of sailing to allow for the stowage of cargo, often presented scenes of chaos. Men, women and children clutching their possessions clawed their way up the sides of the vessels, frequently falling back into the sea where they were left to drown. Some survived only because they were hauled aboard, landed precipitately on deck like fish, by the more helpful crew members. Once down below each found himself or herself part of a seething mass of humanity with barely enough room to turn round. All the steerage passengers were poor, and in addition many were illiterate, filthy and riddled with disease. Their berths were little more than dog kennels, six square feet of space into which it was intended four people should fit. Families were at least spared the humiliation of finding themselves bedded down with complete strangers, a fate reserved for those men and women travelling singly. On most ships lavatories were almost unknown but if they existed, it was in a ratio of one to every hundred passengers, few of whom had little idea of personal hygiene. Sometimes they were situated on deck and therefore useless in rough weather, and in the virtually unventilated cess pit below men, women and children vomited and excreted as well as cooked, ate and slept. By comparison a pig sty represented luxurious living.

An earlier Passenger Act of 1803 had stipulated that ships bound for Canada and America must carry enough food to last for twelve weeks, and it was estimated that each person needed half a pound of meat, usually salt pork, one and a half pounds of biscuits or oatmeal, half a pound of molasses and one gallon of water per day.[25] This was later increased to bread, biscuit and oatmeal totalling seven pounds in weight for each passenger for every week of the voyage, the duration of which was estimated at ten weeks.[26] Rebecca found to her relief that these rations, combined with those bought in Liverpool, allowed her family to be fed adequately, and abandoning the traditional mealtimes of home, she prepared their food whenever the opportunity arose, usually when the other passengers had already eaten, finding it frankly dangerous to compete for space around a fire on a pitching sea.

During the first few days the weather was good, but when the "Home" sailed out of the Irish Sea it ran into a north-westerly gale and very soon began to roll alarmingly on a heavy swell. The ensuing storm proved severe and unnerved even the most hardened of the sailors. For the first time in their lives, the family now experienced the misery of sea-sickness. Weak and ill they huddled together for comfort while the ship creaked alarmingly, her prow pointing high into the sky before crashing back into the all-engulfing waves. Around them the air was full of cries and moans, and the hitherto blasphemous rabble which constituted their fellow travelling companions, fell uninhibitedly to its knees in order to plead for divine intervention. Even in the midst of their own distress this sudden upsurge of religious fervour from their motley companions provided John and Rebecca with much wry amusement. Throughout the night the storm continued unabated and during that time the family, anticipating that the ship would founder at any moment, quietly prayed together. Meanwhile on the deck the shouts of the sailors were occasionally audible as they battled unceasingly in the wind and rain while above it all, Captain Mitchell's voice could be heard, crisply and calmly issuing orders and bringing at least some measure of comfort to the frightened people listening below.

The coming of dawn brought greatly improved conditions although orders were to remain below until the Captain had moved through the ship assuring everyone that the danger was passed. Such consideration gives some indication of his character. Most captains of emigrant vessels contrived to create such intolerable conditions in the steerage that even in the most extreme circumstances they were careful never to set foot below deck themselves. If nothing else his words had the effect of instantly banishing the new-found piety of the emigrants, Rebecca observing with some asperity that the praying stopped as speedily as it had begun. Soon their fellow passengers were dancing, drinking, singing and eating with riotous abandon, religious observance nowhere in evidence. Amazingly the ship had suffered only minimal damage which was swiftly repaired, and although it had been driven considerably off course into the Bay of Biscay, by evening sails were once more unfurled and its course reset.

A vista of sea and sky soon proved of insufficient interest to Rebecca. She began to find the voyage tedious, missing the variety of a country landscape, its sounds, smells and moods. One night whilst on deck enjoying the fresh air, she discovered a full moon, the first familiar sight for many days, and hailed it as an old friend; it seemed inconceivable that the moon of her English childhood should also be present in mid-ocean and she took comfort from its pale presence silvering the surface of the water.

As the days crawled slowly by most of the emigrants were impatient for their first sight of land. Few had any idea of the distance involved in an Atlantic crossing, still less of the length of time it could be expected to take; in fact it was not uncommon for the coast of Ireland to be mistaken for that of America. In the steerage they passed the time exchanging life histories and telling jokes. Some groups combined their rations, cooking and eating together, but natural reserve and a strict sense of economy compelled Rebecca to remain aloof. Beyond the circumstances of their incarceration she and John felt they had little in common with their travelling companions. Instead they maintained a friendly distance, and whenever possible they spent their time on deck enjoying the fresh air and solitude.

On one such occasion alone with her own somewhat sombre thoughts Rebecca managed to avert a catastrophe. Jack, a young stowaway who had somehow escaped detection during the routine inspection after putting out from Liverpool, and had been discovered only when it was too late to turn back, had been set to work his passage in the galley. Here he inadvertently spilled onto the fire a pan of pitch, used for caulking the seams of the ship. As the pitch ignited the wood, Rebecca, noticing that a great deal of smoke was issuing from one of the nearby cabins, raised the alarm. Swarming hastily to the scene the sailors staunched the draught of the chimney with a mattress, forming a chain of water buckets to extinguish the licking flames. In the ensuing melee Rebecca somehow became entangled in ropes near the door to the cabin where, unable to free herself, she was forced to remain, almost asphyxiated by the fumes until the crisis had passed, and the crew had time to notice and release her. The acclaim she subsequently received from the other passengers and the ship's company was no less than she deserved for the danger from fire in old sailing ships was far greater than that from the elements. The merest spark on oak and pine timbers liberally soaked in tar and oil was sufficient to cause an inferno in seconds and many ships, together with a great number of lives, were lost in this way. For the unfortunate Jack, whose arm was quite badly burned, the accident had its advantages. The injury prevented him from working, and even aroused much sympathy amongst the cabin passengers who provided him with replacement clothing.

Within a day or so Rebecca had even further reason to be thankful for her addiction to fresh air. Walking along the deck with John, her attention was suddenly caught by the sight of their eldest son, apparently fast asleep and stretched out along the bowsprit with only a piece of flimsy netting between himself and the ocean. Mute with terror Rebecca could only clutch at her husband's arm to attract his attention. Fortunately his initial reaction which was to shout for assistance from the crew, was suppressed for the child's position was so perilous that if he had been startled and woken suddenly, he might very easily have been dislodged from his perch. Instead, reasoning quickly that it would be better to try to reach the child himself and rouse him gently, he inched his way along the bowsprit with extreme caution while Rebecca, hardly daring to watch, remained on deck, comforted by some of the passengers and the crew. His progress was agonisingly slow and her heart lurched with every roll of the ship expecting at any moment to see her husband and son thrown into the waves. It seemed an eternity before John was able to curl his legs tightly around the slender bowsprit and reach out for the child. Any fears that the boy might take fright and fall were however quite unfounded. Far from being scared by his predicament he appeared completely relaxed, enabling John to concentrate on his own retreat, while he followed confidently on his own. So relieved was Rebecca to see them both safe that her son completely escaped any punishment, and even John's quick temper was curbed. Punishment would probably have made little difference however. John was a naturally adventurous child, and his exploits were to cause John and Rebecca many other anxious moments in the years ahead.

This episode was in fact one reflection of the lack of amusement which shipboard life offered the children although the family tried to make the most of whatever diversion was on hand to help them pass the time. Often they congregated at the rails to watch the flying fish, and it was while they were engrossed in this spectacular display that they noticed an elegant sailing vessel some distance away. In fact the ship was causing the crew considerable concern, Captain Mitchell himself already observing it closely through a telescope. When it was clear that the vessel was indeed advancing on them and rumours of piracy began to circulate on board, the sailors were immediately instructed to prepare the guns for action. As the unknown ship came within range everyone on board the "Home" watched apprehensively. Except for the slap of water on the ships' sides, all was initially unnaturally quiet. Then, from the mainmast of the unknown vessel, a flag broke, a sign of peace, to which the captain swiftly responded, ordering the unfurling of his own national ensign. The situation understood three cheers of relief went up from the deck while over a loud hailer it was soon established that the stranger, originally bound for the West Indies, had lost her position due to storm damage. This situation Captain Mitchell was able to rectify, and amid still more cheers, this time from both ships, the vessel was able to set her new course.

Next day there was even more excitement when land which proved to be the West Indies was sighted. The heat was now intense and the crew erected awnings of sail-cloth to protect the passengers who were all on deck to see for themselves the islands with their attractive beaches, sugar cane and tobacco plantations. The men working beside their huts who paused to watch the ship pass by were the first black men the family had ever seen. Rebecca was enchanted by the beauty of these islands. They seemed to her to represent Paradise and she wished that this was to be their destination. Although this tantalisingly brief glimpse of land meant that the passengers anticipated the appearance of the American coastline even more eagerly, their expectations were short-lived. Once the islands had been passed several days elapsed without further sightings, and the sense of anti-climax made the shipboard routine even more irksome than before. Only when the waiting had become almost unendurable did land appear again, and this time there was no doubt that their long voyage was almost at an end.

Full of relief for their safe arrival but nonetheless apprehensive for their future, Rebecca leaned on the rails, watching their new country enlarge on the horizon. That night the "Home" anchored off New Orleans in the Mississippi delta to await the arrival of the pilot while John, too excited to sleep, stayed on deck to be joined in the early hours by Rebecca. A hundred years earlier there had been nothing here but forest, and the site had been cleared by the French, the town being built by Canadians working alongside slaves and convicts. Now like Manchester, it was entering the golden age of cotton and was about to become the fourth major port in the world. On the following morning, Sunday the 1st November, 1831, the pilot was rowed out by eight sailors, and the "Home" was at last taken safely into harbour, two months and a few days after leaving Liverpool.

CHAPTER VI

Into the Interior

JOHN AND REBECCA'S original intention, to continue the journey up river to St. Louis immediately, was thwarted by the discovery that no steamboat would be sailing from New Orleans for at least twenty four hours. They were therefore obliged to endure the frustrating delay of yet another night on board before they could receive their customs exemption papers from Captain Mitchell, and were able to disembark the following morning. This was a bitter sweet occasion. Although impatient to complete their journey they were nevertheless sad to leave the ship which was their only remaining link with home. The moment of parting however was however somewhat softened by the presentation of small gifts to each of the children, a token of affection from the captain and crew.

Once ashore the family found the streets packed with a jostling throng. They were particularly fascinated by the people, fifty percent of them black, and were deeply shocked to see groups of manacled slaves being driven like cattle through the streets. A further revelation was the Mississippi River, in places a mile and a half wide, against which even the biggest rivers of England seemed mere streams. To the Burlands it seemed like a miniature inland ocean. At moorings was a large number of small craft, many of them quaint flatboats which closely resembled upturned box lids, and which were therefore eminently suited to the shallow water. Up to seventy feet long and twelve feet wide, with a central portion roofed over to provide crude living accommodation, they were used by some emigrants to travel upstream, and as they were usually laden with poultry and cattle, were consequently known as "arks".[27] Later, when they had become established in the backwoods, in the spring the settlers loaded them with their produce such as corn and pork, and the flatboat would be re-launched and the current relied on to carry the cargo downstream to the markets of New Orleans.

Before arranging the next part of their journey, John and Rebecca changed their remaining sovereigns into dollars. Since leaving Barwick they had spent £23 which to them seemed to be an enormous sum, and they were therefore relieved to discover that the fare to St. Louis on the main deck of the steamboat where the cargo was also stored, would be only four dollars. In the very humid weather conditions the passengers found this mode of travel infinitely preferable to the stuffy and more expensive cabins on the upper deck. The voyage up river which probably lasted for about three weeks[28] proved on the whole to be most enjoyable. For all of that time they were happy to spend the day cooking meals, and watching the scenery slide by. The fertile river banks were quite flat, and the farmer's eye in John was able to observe the sugar cane and cotton plantations which were well cultivated, and apparently endowed with a plentiful supply of labour. It was a time of great economic expansion in the deep south due largely to imported slave labour, which particularly distressed Rebecca. In fact the presence of the black workers was solely responsible for marring her appreciation of the countryside, reminding her of the toll of human suffering exacted by the land.

Along the route there were frequent stops for refuelling. Steamboats consumed a vast quantity of the wood which was abundant at the river side, and which deck passengers collected in return for a reduction in their fare.[29] During one such halt one of the passengers approached a man sitting by his hut to ask if he might take some fruit from a nearby tree. The man readily agreed but when the unfortunate passenger stepped up onto what appeared to be a box, it collapsed under his weight. As the top splintered the man leapt to his feet and fled in terror, understandable for the box in question proved to be a beehive, the enraged occupants of which lost no time in venting their indignation on the intruder who sped back to the boat at the double to the amusement of all on board. As they progressed further upriver the countryside became wilder. Date and plantain trees gave way to vast areas of forest with intermittent glimpses of the prairie, and occasionally John and Rebecca spotted settler's shacks surrounded by small patches of crudely tilled ground. This forbidding landscape was not exactly the Utopia they had been led to believe awaited them, and despite the optimism of their fellow passengers, they began to feel more than a little apprehensive.

In times of trouble Rebecca frequently found her salvation in occupation. Her willingness to help both with the sick and with other people's children had ensured that since leaving New Orleans she had been cast in the role of ship's matron, and her wide knowledge of herbs and their uses had stood everyone in good stead. For her assistance the other passengers paid in kind so that the family never went hungry and indeed lived well on fowls, rice and coffee in addition to food which they were able to acquire along the way. Not everyone was so appreciative however. One night when the children were safely tucked up in bed, and the two of them had also retired for the night, she to sleep and John, as usual, to lie awake pondering their uncertain future, a crew member knowing them to be new settlers, began to search under Rebecca's pillow for the money which he knew they must have. In fact the purse in question was actually under John's pillow, and it was he who told the intruder that he would give him whatever he was looking for. Startled at being caught in the act, and even further disconcerted by the reaction of his victim, the would-be-thief fled empty handed. When Rebecca awoke having been disturbed by the commotion, she offered up a prayer for their deliverance. The loss of the purse was unthinkable containing as it did every penny they possessed. Determined to take no further risks, the next morning John arranged for the captain to take custody of it for the duration of the voyage.

At noon on a bleak November day, twelve days after their departure from New Orleans the family reached St. Louis. Named after Louis IX of France, the city had been part of the United States for a little under thirty years, and with the advent of the steamboat era in 1817 had become one of America's busiest ports, and the centre of the fur trade. In 1831 it had a population of only about 5,000 but its situation near the confluence of the Missouri, Mississippi and Illinois Rivers meant that it was suitably poised for a period of rapid economic growth. As usual Rebecca was prevented from being able to explore by the presence of the children although by now she had almost become used to being left on her own in strange places, sometimes for quite lengthy periods, while John arranged the next stage of their journey. However she rarely found the wait boring, and that at St. Louis was no exception. As well as steamboats constantly arriving and departing from the crowded quayside, the river itself teemed with small boats piled so high with people and produce that they appeared to be in imminent danger of sinking. Farmers unloaded cereals and livestock, trappers carried piles of pelts shoulder high to the nearest trading post, and other new pioneer families like the Burlands also sought out the boats which would take them nearer to their destinations.

When John returned the family was able to board a second boat almost immediately, although this was considerably less comfortable than the steamer from New Orleans, and to add further to their discomfort the weather had suddenly turned bitterly cold. Fortunately they were now within a hundred and twenty miles of their goal, and relieved to learn that this final stage along the Illinois River would be accomplished in a mere twenty four hours. By the time the boat slowed and then stopped at their destination, Phillips Ferry, it was quite dark and impossible to see the shore. The family clustered at the rails while a small boat was lowered into the water allowing John to climb down and distribute their boxes, mattresses and Rebecca's rocking chair. Rebecca then lowered each of the children down to him before herself climbing into the inky darkness, and they were rowed ashore to what they had been led to believe was the promised land.

Despite George's letter they hardly knew what to expect. A town probably, certainly a settlement of some size where there would be someone to direct them to George's home just a couple of miles away. Instead, once ashore, alone and in the blackness of the night, John and Rebecca gazed round blankly, unclear what to do next. The river bank in either direction was completely deserted, and as far as they could see there was neither jetty nor building of any description. Instead they were surrounded by dense woodland totally unlike anything they had anticipated; in fact until they had arrived in St. Louis it had not occurred to them that they would reach the end of their journey in the middle of the night. Seeing each others mutual despair they broke down and wept, while the four older children, adopting the mood of their parents, joined in. With the exception of baby William, warmly wrapped in his mother's arms and blissfully unaware of their dilemma, they were cold, hungry and frightened. For three months over 7,000 miles they had eagerly anticipated this moment. Now they were too disappointed and exhausted to be able to think any further. Certainly their first impressions were not those of the "land flowing with milk and honey" which George had so lyrically described.

John was the first to recover at least some of his composure. It was clear that he would have to go in search of some kind of shelter or to find someone able to offer them assistance, and that would be quicker and simpler if he once again went alone while Rebecca stayed with the children. Reluctant though she was to acknowledge the wisdom of this, she watched with some trepidation as her husband vanished into the woods. Shivering from a combination of fear and the penetrating cold, she rallied the children into action at the same time trying to conceal from them the consternation she felt. Wrapping each of them in a blanket as a protection from the keen frost and sitting them in a row on one of the mattresses, she knelt before them to say a short prayer. Then, still striving to maintain an outward show of calm, she seated herself alongside to await her husband's return.

It was fortunate that she and the children were unaware that the land on which they had come ashore was still regarded by the Sauk Indians as their own personal territory. Even without that knowledge they still found their surroundings daunting. The night sky was black and clear, the stars glittering and shimmering with an extraordinary brilliance, and before them the deep, wide waters of the Illinois River swirled by in menacing silence. In the woods the stillness was intermittently rent by the unmistakable shriek of an owl, and the rustling of unidentifiable creatures which they all profoundly hoped were small and harmless. When eventually these noises were supplanted by the more mundane barking of dogs, and when it became apparent that those dogs were accompanied by John and another man, Rebecca's relief was great.

Ten years earlier, Andrew Phillips had come to Illinois from Kentucky with his parents, Nimrod and Nancy, but in recent months Nimrod had died having bequeathed the ferry to his son. Now Andrew quickly took command of the situation. Promising to send a waggon the next day to collect their heavy luggage, he led the way down a long, narrow track between tall trees to a log cabin deep in the heart of the wood. There his mother waited at the door to greet her unexpected guests, and to offer them refreshment which apart from a hot drink, they were all too exhausted to accept. Meanwhile the men laid straw mattresses on the floor before a blazing fire, and John and Rebecca thankfully settled themselves for the remainder of the night, the children lying between them.

The Burlands remained with the Phillips family for three days but although Rebecca was deeply grateful to Nancy for her hospitality, she found that she was not a woman who inspired her affection. A tough, talkative little person much addicted to her pipe of tobacco, she lost little time in making it clear that she expected her guests to pay in full for their stay even though they were in fact still eating their own provisions, and on one occasion invited Rebecca to feed the children on the water in which she had boiled some cabbage. It was with some asperity that Rebecca refused, informing their hostess that her children were unaccustomed to such a diet. In fairness to Nancy however, it could not have been easy to take into her cramped cabin a family of total strangers, especially when that family included four lively children and a six month old baby. With the exception of a small loft, the cabin had no upper floor and the ground floor consisted only of two large rooms separated by ill-fitting timbers so that it was possible to see through the cracks. The windowless outer walls were constructed from strong lengths of timber interlocking at the corners, their joints sealed only with clay, and at the end of the building stood a fire on the stone floor beneath a large and bizarre chimney piece constructed from stones off the land which were cemented roughly with mud. In one of these rooms a few planks nailed together and supported by the wall of the house served as a sideboard, while in the centre of the room a kitchen table was covered with a piece of coarse brown calico. There were also four chairs with caned seats, two stools and a bench, some trenchers and tin mugs, and a candlestick made from an ear of corn. Suspended from the roof were bunches of herbs, a couple of guns, some hams smoked black and two or three sides of beef. One corner of this room was occupied by farming implements while in the other was a loom on which the family wove their own clothes. Beneath two beds were kept several jars of honey. In a clay-walled cellar beneath one of the rooms, Rebecca saw tubs of lard and a large amount of the home-produced tobacco of which Nancy was so fond. During their time with the Phillips family, John and Rebecca were initiated into some of the ways of their adopted country amongst which was the fact that it was considered impolite for them to remain at the table once they had finished eating because it might imply that they had had insufficient to eat. To their surprise they also discovered that all Americans whatever their status expected to be addressed as 'sir' or 'madam'.

John meanwhile had at last managed to contact George Bickerdike who had luckily proved to be a friend of Andrew's sister, Ann. Although he returned from their first meeting in a strangely uncommunicative mood, Rebecca was delighted that he had at last managed to make contact with their old friend. It was good to feel more secure and to be able to relish the prospect of leaving Nancy Phillips to set up in a home of their own. So that they might move their belongings, George had sent his sledge pulled by a couple of oxen and their hostess, duly paid in full, stood in the doorway of her cabin to watch them leave. As the children once again scrambled onto the top of their possessions, she was actually seen to shed a few parting tears; perhaps like those of Rebecca, they were purely of relief and thankfulness. Unfortunately Rebecca's own sense of relief was short-lived. Arriving at George's cabin, which despite his absence was unlocked, they found that it bore all the hallmarks of a penurious bachelor, containing only the minimum of furniture which included a bolster on a rough plank serving as a bed. Moreover the walls which were unsealed meant that the occupants were virtually exposed to the elements and it was now only too easy to understand the reason for John's earlier lack of enthusiasm. During their first night, Rebecca was so bitterly cold that John had to improvise a hot water bottle from a heated flat iron wrapped in a flannel. Clearly the need for a home of their own was imperative, but in the matter of land purchase George was of very little help. Evidently everything was not nearly as rosy as he would have had everyone at home believe, and he was now too preoccupied with his own problems to pay much attention to those of others. Indeed Rebecca privately voiced the opinion that the condition of his clothing was so inconsistent with standards of decency, it would have been impossible for him to venture far from his cabin even if he had wanted to.

New settlers found the acquisition of land a complex business. In 1831 when the Burlands arrived in Illinois the government was still in the process of banishing the indigenous Indian population by driving it further and further west. Various tribes were known to inhabit the area. As well as the Sauk Indians who lived along the banks of the Mississippi between Rock Island and St. Louis, the Winnebago and Kickapoo hunted bison on the prairies. In 1832 many Indians perished during the Black Hawk War when they were trapped by the United States Army at Bad Ax Creek further north in Wisconsin. Some attempted to escape by plunging into the deep wide waters of the Mississippi, but many of them never succeeded in attaining the safety of the Iowa shore.[30] Once the Indians had been dispossessed of their land, laws were established to govern its distribution. Having been surveyed it was divided into townships each comprising six square miles or 3,840 acres, and these in turn were split into square mile sections of 640 acres, or quarter sections of 160 acres; there were even plots as small as 40 acres, a system of land division which is still evident in the geometric landscape of the present mid-West. The sale of the allotments was handled by the Federal Land Office, a purchaser being required to swear on oath that the land was not already in the process of being improved. Anyone making a false declaration on this score found himself heavily fined and his purchase invalidated.

John was in the process of familiarising himself with this system when he had a visit from a squatter known as Oakes. Ostensibly calling at the Bickerdike cabin to sell some freshly killed venison, in the course of conversation Oakes revealed that he also wished to sell land on which he had already made some improvements, and to settle elsewhere. He had no legal title to his land having simply pre-empted a plot and broken up enough land to provide some crops, supplementing his diet and income by hunting and trapping. Once a settler had obtained a pre-emption he was free to make improvements for a period of four years. Only when this period had elapsed did the pre-emption acts of the early 1830's require him to pay in full for his plot at the local land office. The price of land was $2.50 per acre and if during this time the settler failed to amass the necessary capital, he was left with no alternative but to witness the dispersal of the land with the improvements he had made at the local land sale.[31] Frequent changes of location were therefore commonplace among settlers and it was rare for them to remain for life on their first holding.

The following day John and Rebecca eagerly visited him to view the eighty acres which were available. Situated in an area of woodland, the soil was black in colour and light in texture, more fertile than anything they could have imagined, and vastly superior to that found on the prairies. The forest, rich in ash and walnut, cherry and hickory, oak and mulberry would provide them with essential building materials as well as kindling for a fire and mast for a pig. In addition the cabin was pleasantly situated on a hillside above a vital stream of crystal clear water. Oakes also showed them the corner stones, large boulders which marked the boundary of his land, and four hundred fine sugar maple trees. A prudent settler only ploughed up just as much land as he could afford to cultivate at any one time and Oakes had been no exception. So far he had broken up twelve acres of the least wooded land, three acres of the best having been sown with wheat while a further nine were prepared for sowing with Indian corn or maize, and with oats in the spring.

Desperately anxious to have a place of their own, John and Rebecca reached an agreement quickly, the following day paying Oakes the sixty dollars he was asking for his house, his improvements and some of his sugar-making utensils. Later John rode to the land office in Quincy handing over a further hundred dollars and signing the ledger, receiving in return the title deeds of their first real home, officially recorded in the registers as the north east quarter of the north east quarter of Section 6, township 5 S, R. 2 W of the fourth P.M.,[32] a prosaic definition which in no way rendered its possession less sweet. In more human terms they were now settled in the Big Blue Creek country of Pike County, three miles north of the small settlement of Detroit, Illinois and three miles south west of Valley City, the proud owners of a log cabin standing on a sloping hillside with eighty acres of good land. Thus, the first part of their dream had been accomplished.

CHAPTER VII

Gaining a Foothold

ANXIOUS TO ESTABLISH themselves in their new home, their first priority was to lay in a supply of food for the scanty supply of provisions bought in New Orleans was by now almost finished, and they were all hungry. Moreover they were very much aware that at any time the weather may worsen thus cutting them off from vital supplies. At first milk was supplied to them by Mr. Paddock, their nearest neighbour whose land adjoined their own, but soon John was able to buy a cow and a calf from Mr. Oakes for fourteen dollars, and these he turned out onto the stubble of part of a cornfield which he had bought from Paddock and reaped himself. In addition he also paid twenty dollars for a mare, and at a corn mill some two and a half miles away, he obtained a bushel of ground Indian corn for thirty cents. Although this was considerably cheaper than wheaten flour, it had a bitter taste which rendered it far less palatable, and Rebecca had to use all her ingenuity to make it more appetising. Undeterred by a lack of yeast she mixed a "sad" bread dough, baking it in a skillet, a shallow iron pan with a lid which she thrust deep into the heart of the glowing fire. She also found that when it was cooked with boiling salted water, the corn made a very satisfying Hasty pudding with which to follow the last of the venison they had bought from Oakes. Once the venison was finished, John killed a couple of pigs.

The essential expenses so far incurred meant that they had little money left when they all began to suffer from an irritating rash. Locally known as Illinois mange it was variously attributed to the change of water, rotting vegetation on newly-ploughed land, or decaying fish on the beds of the rivers. Significantly however it was a common condition amongst new settlers, and it therefore seems more likely that in the dirty and over-crowded conditions which prevailed on board ship, the immigrants had contracted scabies. Whatever their origin, the spots itched unbearably causing much distress, particularly to the children, and Rebecca had reluctantly to allocate some of their remaining funds for the purchase of sulphur at the nearest store. However, while this expenditure quickly cured the condition it also meant that other everyday items had to be done without or made at home. Despite a lack of skill John managed to make some stools and a bench, fashioning a table from a tree trunk and a couple of rough planks; in addition the two of them managed to build some crude bedsteads for the children. Each evening when the more exhausting daily chores were finished, Rebecca made clothes for the family despite the fact that her output was severely restricted by the shortage of daylight in the windowless cabin. With neither moulds nor tallow to manufacture candles, she had eventually to improvise by setting a piece of rag in a lump of lard, and by this method found that she could see quite well both to sew and to read. Unfortunately the heat resulted in much broken crockery which they could ill afford to replace, a problem Rebecca eventually overcame by substituting the more durable kettle lid for the saucer.

Soap was another very necessary ingredient which also had to be made at home, a technique which Rebecca had learned during her stay with Nancy Phillips. Ashes from the fire were placed in a wooden trough while boiling water poured onto them provided a solution of potash. This was boiled down, a second solution was added to the first and the whole quantity was boiled down again to about one third of the original. At this stage the solution was so caustic as to be extremely dangerous, and very careful handling was required. Only when pig's entrails had been stirred into the mixture did it assume the consistency of soft soap, and could safely be poured into a jar ready for use.

While Rebecca struggled with domestic problems, John had his own difficulties with the stock. The mare bought from Oakes apparently preferred the company of other horses to cattle, repeatedly jumping the fences and causing John to waste much valuable time recapturing her. Eventually he decided that it would save time, and would certainly cause less trouble, if he exchanged her for another which, although of vastly inferior quality to the first, more than redeemed herself by proving to be in foal. When he was not tending the stock or chopping firewood for the house, much of his time was spent fencing their property. Supplies of wood were fortunately plentiful and it did not take him long to master the technique of building American-style fences which were considerably easier to construct than their English counterparts. The sub-zero temperatures of winter made it easy to split the wood and the prepared rails were then laid on the ground, their ends overlapping to form a cross, and a post hammered into each angle of the cross thus securing the lengths. Other rails continued to be added until the required height, often as much as nine feet, had been achieved.

Soon after he had first completed the fencing John was surprised to discover two strange horses grazing on his land. Somewhat baffled by their presence, his fences having been found to be in good order, he turned them off into the woods in the hope that they would find their own way home. The next day however they had returned and it was obvious that someone was actively responsible for their reappearance. No sooner had the trespassers been turned out yet again than John found himself confronted by a tall and extremely truculent stranger who had evidently been concealed nearby, and who now declared that the animals not only belonged to him but furthermore had every right to remain. In the ensuing argument John received a vicious punch on the head and was threatened with still further violence. Although perfectly capable of defending himself, he had no wish to become involved in an unseemly brawl; nor, considering the vulnerability of his family, did he wish to run the risk of more serious injury. Declining to pursue the matter he later learned that the stranger, identified as a Mr. Brevet, was known to be a violent man who would have used a knife if John had offered further resistance. When, some weeks later, both he and his animals vanished, it was to the relief, not only of the Burlands but of everyone in the neighbourhood where it transpired he was universally unpopular.

The Burlands were appalled by the savagery of their first winter in Illinois. The river became unnavigable having frozen solid in a single night, the pork they had stored away could only be hacked into suitably sized joints with difficulty, milk froze as soon as it left the cow, and all their water had to be thawed over the fire which was never allowed to die out. The bedding they had taken with them from England was quite inadequate, and there was no prospect of being able to afford any more. Most of what they possessed was used to cover the children but it still provided insufficient warmth and they suffered bitterly from both the intense cold and the pain from severe chillblains. In Barwick, Rebecca would have treated these with salt and a raw onion but in Illinois only the salt was readily to hand. Until the following summer when she would have the opportunity of growing and gathering some of the many herbs she was accustomed to using for medicinal purposes, she just had to hope that her family would not develop anything too dire.

Vast quantities of wood were constantly in demand to feed the fire and although every spare moment John had was spent in chopping the hickory logs which burned so brightly, there never seemed to be enough for their needs. Young John helped as much as he was able and the strenuous activity at least kept the two of them warm. Like all pioneers the Burlands soon became aware of the importance of never allowing their fire to die out, and a large green log known as a backlog lay at the back of the fireplace where its sap ensured its slow burning, thus allowing it to act as a backing for the drier wood. When the backlog eventually became dry itself, it was then rolled forward and burned, and a new backlog added. On one occasion Rebecca allowed the backlog to dry out and burn up, and young John had to be sent out into a snowstorm to fetch live embers from George Bickerdike two miles away. These he transported in his mittened hands, the live ember at the centre being insulated by ashes above and below.

Through it all Rebecca's spirit apparently remained indomitable. With John out working the land or exploring their surrounding territory for hours at a time, she was often completely alone except for the children, and opportunities for her to meet people were virtually nonexistent. Indeed their encounter with Mr. Brevet had only served to make them wary of strangers so that as far as possible they kept themselves to themselves. Often on these winter nights she enjoyed standing at the door of their cabin admiring the frosty glitter of the stars and listening apprehensively to the tortured howls of the wolves away in the forest. Sometimes these creatures came right up to the cabin looking for food, a young pig perhaps, and then the children shrank down under their thin coverings, huddling together for comfort and poking their fingers into their ears in a vain attempt to obliterate the eerie sounds outside.

Coming on the heels of their rigorous journey the vicious winter understandably quenched their spirits considerably. The stocks of food hoarded in November had proved to be inadequate, they were unable to sell any of their cattle because the milk was necessary for the family, and most of their land still remained uncultivated. It was also a difficult time for the children. Unlike winter in England it was too cold for them to go outside, and they had no toys or games with which to amuse themselves indoors. The only book in the cabin was the family Bible, zealously guarded by their parents and used by Rebecca to teach all of them to read and write. She also taught them some simple arithmetic finding them quick and eager to learn. Once lessons were over for the day, young John mostly occupied himself by helping his father while Hannah was especially useful to Rebecca, cooking, sewing and generally attending to the needs of the younger children.

One of their great burdens at this time was their inability to attend any form of organised worship, their nearest preaching house being about five miles away. Nevertheless, as befitted a family of staunch Methodist conviction, they somehow contrived to keep Sunday a strict day of rest. While Rebecca held baby William on her lap, the older children sat on a bench listening to John read aloud from the Bible. Afterwards they all joined together to sing the hymns they remembered from home. Such makeshift devotions were however a poor substitute for the regular church attendance to which they had been accustomed. In the frontier lands of America at the time a rugged band of men known as circuit riders paid visits on many of the settlers. The Blue Creek country of Pike County was part of the Atlas Circuit where three preachers in particular were well established. Lewis Allen and Jesse Elledge, both relatives of the legendary American hero, Daniel Boone, had been joined in about 1826 by the renowned preacher, Jesse Walker. Riding alone from settlement to settlement these men of firm conviction fought their way daily through dense black forests where the sun rarely if ever penetrated, across unbroken prairie grasslands and around swamps regardless of the weather conditions for a salary of $80. Those they visited were not always welcoming, some indeed were downright hostile, but the dedicated circuit rider was not easily deterred. Surrounded by people many of whom lived more like primitive savages than civilised human beings, his only weapons a Bible and a hymn book, he fearlessly introduced the Gospel into their midst and in so doing was no less courageous than those missionaries who sought to convert the heathen tribes of Africa. In some homes he was ridiculed and beaten up, in others he was given the warmest possible welcome. The uncertainty was as much a part of his life as the freezing cold and the melting heat, the crushing loneliness and the spiritual communion. Sometimes when the harvest was over, a rider would let it be known that he was to preach in the cabin of a member of his flock. Word was then passed along the creek to those of the appropriate persuasion, and the majority of settlers flocked to take part in these infrequent acts of worship, listening avidly to the sermons and singing lustily, not only during the service but also afterwards on the lonely trek home. Such an event was a great occasion in the lives of the faithful, remembered and cherished until the next time.

As the weather conditions deteriorated even further, the family found that still more demands were made on their powers of ingenuity and improvisation. In the freezing temperatures their butter refused to "come", the cream having frozen solid, a difficulty eventually surmounted by keeping the churn close to the fire and churning both milk and cream together. Despite such measures however, butter making became an increasingly onerous duty undertaken less and less often during the winter months, until eventually it proved simpler to abandon it altogether until the warmer weather returned. In the spring of 1832 however their hopes rose afresh. The cruel frost slowly relinquished its hold on the land, and while the icicles festooning the house dripped monotonously onto the reappearing earth, the children watched from the cabin door, eager to be out of doors. When the time came Rebecca was only too glad to let them go revelling in her own freedom as well as in theirs.

At the beginning of March it was time for their first sugar harvest. A fall of soft, wet snow which made the branches droop beneath the heavy weight so that they looked like an icing sugar fantasy was, George Bickerdike explained, a "sugar snow" which would delay the trees from coming into leaf and so allow the sap to run for longer. Having acquired the necessary equipment from his predecessor there was no need for John to delay, and he made incisions with an auger in the trunks of the huge trees. Tubes made from the branches of the sumac tree, each measuring about an inch in diameter, were then hammered into the holes and the liquid drained off into wooden buckets, all of which were subsequently emptied into a huge copper hanging from a cross-beam between two trees. A fire lit beneath, the liquid was boiled and skimmed repeatedly until it reached the consistency of thin treacle when it could be eaten on Hasty pudding or pancakes. The children loved it best of all poured onto a dish of snow where it solidified into a chunk of sweet, chewy wax. Once this stage had been reached the remainder of the sap continued to be boiled until it started to grain. Then speed was of the essence, the fire having to be raked away from the pot quickly, and the syrup poured into containers to set as dark brown maple syrup.

That first year John and Rebecca did extremely well from "sugaring off" as it was known. Altogether they made three hundredweight of sugar and a barrel of molasses, a most welcome harvest and enough to enable them to do some much needed shopping. Their local storekeeper, a Mr. Varley, lived a few miles away serving a wide but very thinly populated area. Many of the local storekeepers combined their businesses with saw and corn milling, processing the settler's harvest and then despatching it downriver to St. Louis and New Orleans. Their small cabins were invariably lined from floor to ceiling with every conceivable requirement including food, spirits, tobacco, cutlery, crockery and farming implements, cloth, medicines, haberdashery, skins, guns and ammunition. However between the shopkeeper and his customer money rarely changed hands, the latter taking his produce along for valuation after which he was allowed to make purchases up to that value. John and Rebecca's sugar harvest was valued at seven to eight cents a pound which they set about spending prudently. It has been said that 'The farm equipment of the pioneer of the 1830's was both simple and limited in amount. A waggon or cart, a couple of plows, a harrow, axe, shovel, scythe, cradle, fork, and rake - these were the essentials. Add a pair of oxen, with yoke and chain, or a team of horses and their harness, and the farm-maker was tolerably well fixed. He could purchase this minimum of equipment and farm stock in the 1830's for $300 or less'.[33] Needless to say such expenditure was way beyond the Burland's reach. Since leaving Barwick they had spent approximately £30 on travel and £40 on land. Now all that was left to them was some £14. Instead they contented themselves with three hoes and a Yankee axe, the latter considerably larger and broader than its English counterpart, as well as some Indian corn for seed, more meal and a fresh supply of coffee.

Keeping a family of seven adequately fed was an eternal problem for Rebecca. Generally they lived on the unpalatable corn, bread, milk and coffee supplemented with whatever John, who had a fowling piece but no rifle, was able to shoot or trap. Rabbits which were in plentiful supply were a welcome addition to the pot, and some quails, which he caught while they were feeding on the Indian corn, proved to be excellent eating. Every day John came across many birds whose identity was unknown to him and it was one of these which provided them with an incident they later came to find amusing despite the fact that at the time it caused them great embarrassment. For some weeks John had been stalking something which he took to be a turkey and which had proved to be exceptionally elusive. Eventually, and only as a result of great patience and determination his attempts were successful, and he was able to bear home his trophy proudly. Rebecca was especially grateful. George Bickerdike, having presumably by this time acquired sufficient funds to equip himself with new trousers, had been invited to eat with them on the following day, and the problem of what they should offer him had been much preoccupying her. Although their diet had improved a little since the early days it still lacked variety, and this unexpected delicacy would be a more than welcome contribution to the table. Like a pair of excited children they prepared the bird together and popped it into the pot scarcely able to contain their delight at the prospect of serving their guest with such a tempting dish. Indeed, as soon as George arrived they lost no time in regaling him with the details of their prize, thus arousing his suspicions which an inspection of the head and feet protruding from the pot, quickly confirmed. The "turkey" was in fact a buzzard, and therefore quite unfit for human consumption. As a sadly deflated John removed his offering to the yard, Rebecca cast around for a suitable alternative finding only the monotonous Indian corn pudding. It is unlikely however that there were any complaints from their guest who must have been more than thankful for his narrow escape. In fact George's own knowledge of the indigenous bird population may also have been limited. While he was probably correct that the bird was a carrion eater, it is more likely that it was in fact a turkey vulture, common in North America and so called because like the conventional turkey it had a bald head. This was in fact the last occasion on which John and Rebecca entertained their friend as a bachelor. On the 22nd May, 1832 George married Ann Phillips, surrounded by members of the bride's family and a small group of friends and other settlers including the Burlands The bride's uncle, Thomas, who as a deacon of the church was licensed to offici-ate, performed the service in the Phillips' cabin, and afterwards the couple took up residence in George's spartan house where Ann had the daunting and unenviable task of trying to create a comfortable and welcoming home.

In the early spring the corn they had bought with the land and husbanded so carefully was exhausted. However in the woods fresh grass was beginning to show through, and the cattle and the in-foal mare could at last be turned out. Despite allowing their stock to run free on common land they rarely lost an animal, the bull generally wearing a bell round his neck so that he could be heard easily. In the unlikely event of a beast attaching itself to another herd, its brand mark was publicised at the local mill, and if it remained unclaimed after a year it was permitted to remain with the finder.

Although March was traditionally considered to be the ideal time for the planting of corn, the acquisition of seed from the local store placed John in something of a quandary. As yet they had nothing with which to prepare the land; indeed even if they had had a plough it would have been impossible to harness their only horse which as well as being old, was also in foal. The corn was already overdue for sowing and if they did not get it into the ground immediately, the season would be finished and their cattle would starve during the following winter. They eventually solved their dilemma by adopting the farming tech-niques of biblical days. John, Rebecca and young John, each armed with one of the new hoes, spent three successive gruelling weeks stab-bing and slashing the ground in order to break up and loosen the soil.

Without a harrow they could not hope to prepare it efficiently for seed, but instead they drew crosses in the soil, bored a hole at the centre of the cross, dropped in a few seeds and stamped down the sods, back-breaking labour which only ceased when the rains came and they were obliged to be satisfied with the four completed acres. Small wonder that Rebecca ever afterwards declared the sowing of seed to be the hardest task of all on the land.

Spring and autumn were renowned for their heavy rainfall and Rebecca was frankly terrified by the accompanying electrical storms. Quite unlike anything she had ever witnessed in England, the fact that they occurred mostly at night made them all the more frightening. The wind roared and howled through the trees, lightening ripped the world apart illuminating the turbulent scene in an eerie yellow glow while one deafening peal of thunder followed immediately upon another. As torrential rain lashed against the walls of the log cabin and the ground vibrated, the family gathered together for prayer and reassurance much as they had done on board ship, but this time fearing for the fabric of their home which seemed so insubstantial in contrast to the stout stone farmhouse they had left behind in Yorkshire. Athough not prone to exaggeration, Rebecca complained that during these storms her '...senses were completely disordered...',[34] and for a while afterwards she dreaded their return, finding herself quickly startled by even the slightest noise. It was in fact to be many years before she overcame her fear altogether and by then, although the trees around the cabin were frequently struck by lightening, she had come to realise that the storms were actually more annoying than dangerous.

With the worst of the inclement weather over they would have liked to attend the prayer meetings held by the local Methodists but their clothing they considered too disreputable, retribution Rebecca claimed for her earlier scathing criticism of George's attire. This restriction cast a bleak shadow over their days but they were a little cheered by the relatively mild weather which brought other benefits. In the middle of May they discovered firstly that the first tender green shoots of corn had started to emerge, and secondly that their mare had dropped her foal. The children gathered round to admire the little filly, captivated by its fragile beauty, and John congratulated himself on his bargain. Unfortunately his pleasure was short-lived. Some days later he found the mare lying on the bed of the dried-up river, apparently unable to get up. The family combined all their efforts to haul her out with ropes, and although at first she seemed none the worse for her experience, her foal later came to the door of the cabin whinneying piteously, and led them back to the same place where this time the mare was dead. Luckily her foal lived on, becoming strong and healthy, and eventually proving to be a valuable brood mare.

Summer evening walks provided further disturbing incidents. One evening Rebecca and John, alone in the dusk on a woodland path, noticed what they took to be sparks of fire flitting through the air ahead of them. Intrigued by this strange sight, they were unable to arrive at any logical explanation despite watching for some time. Eventually, assuming it to be some sort of superhuman phenomenon, they hurried home fearfully. Only later while expressing their bewilderment to a visitor were they abashed to discover that they had merely had their first experience of fireflies, or light bugs as they were more commonly called.

In early summer there was a great deal of work to be done on the land and Rebecca began to work alongside her husband. Already they had three acres of wheat and half a rood of potatoes but they pressed on to take in still more land adding to that already broken up by Oates. In sharp contrast to the prairie land which was thickly matted with roots and grass, and needed a special prairie breaking plough, once wooded land had been cleared it tilled fairly easily, and while John worked at felling trees and grubbing up roots with a mattock, Rebecca and young John helped by collecting up the brushwood and carrying it back to the cabin for the fire. By the end of May they had added another four acres of cleared land to their holding and were able to begin fencing off an eight acre field which they were determined to plough the following season.

Their financial situation was still however far from stable. Despite their frugality, funds were very short and they found it necessary to resort to the purchase of meal on credit. Although this debt amounted only to one dollar, it was the first they had incurred since their arrival in Illinois and it caused them much embarrassment. Moreover while Varley, the storekeeper, was only too happy to allow them to take whatever they needed, confident that he could trust them to reimburse him in due course, the miller proved to be altogether less obliging, giving them short weight as soon as he learned of their straitened circumstances Despite the anger this aroused in John, he accepted the slight without comment fearing that a complaint might only aggravate the situation, and indeed result in the miller's refusal to supply them at all. As things stood the meal they had been given would help to keep them in bread for six weeks at least, and by that time their own wheat would be reaped. It was indeed fortunate that John was unable to foresee the events of the days ahead.

CHAPTER VIII

Progress and Problems

AS THE END OF June approached John began to make preparations for the harvest. They had no sickles of their own and because they cost more than a dollar each, had so far not been able to afford any. John borrowed two from George but on the way home, he tripped over a log concealed in the long grass falling directly onto one of the blades and receiving a deep wound to the knee. Bleeding profusely and still a mile from home, Rebecca had to improvise a tourniquet so that he was eventually able to continue to the cabin where she bathed the wound, applying herbs and a bandage. Despite these measures the wound subsequently became infected, the leg swelled, and John developed a high fever. For two days he took only sips of coffee and became increasingly weak. Rebecca, concerned and frightened, could only watch and wait. For a time it seemed quite likely that she was about to lose not only her husband but also her sole means of support, and although she tried to conceal her fear from the children, the gravity of the situation did not escape young John who knelt at his father's side begging him to live. Rebecca herself had almost given up hope of any improvement when their luck turned and the fever broke. Within a week sensation in the affected limb had returned to normal, and John was sufficiently recovered to sit on a stool propped up against the cabin wall with pillows at his back, a change Rebecca felt was nothing short of a miracle, and proof if she had needed any that God was indeed looking after them.

She was still rejoicing when she realised that the demands of the harvest could be ignored no longer. Their wheat was by now more than ready for reaping and it was clear that if they were not to starve in the coming winter, she would have to harvest the crop herself. Consequently it fell to nine year old Hannah to remain at home caring for her father, younger sisters and brother, while John accompanied his mother to the field. Hour after hour the two of them worked together, grimly determined to finish the job, almost fainting in the heat, bodies aching, hands blistered and driven to distraction by swarms of mosquitoes. Prairie dwellers were generally unaffected by these pests but in the spring and autumn they were common in the woodlands where, apart from the pain and itching caused by their bites, they made sleep impossible. Rebecca often spent nights repeatedly fanning them from her face with a handkerchief, and sometimes when they were particularly troublesome, John built a smoky fire in the open doorway of the cabin in an effort to discourage them although inevitably they returned as soon as the fire died down.

By the end of the week the wheat had been cut, but in the blazing heat it was drying out far too quickly and with no waggon at their disposal, Rebecca had to set about devising her own means of transportation. By arranging the sheaves on top of two poles stretcher fashion, being careful to place more at her own end than at the other, they were able to bring home a total of three acres of wheat while John, at last able to walk with the aid of a stick, came to the door of the cabin and instructed them in the complicated art of stacking the sheaves. Once fully recovered, his first task was to thresh the wheat with a flail, winnowing with the wind in the absence of the appropriate machine. The grain was then shovelled into sacks and a sample taken to Varley who offered them a choice of payment of either half a dollar a bushel, or a few cents more in barter. Opting for the latter, John borrowed a waggon and oxen from a neighbour and delivered fifty bushels of the hard-won wheat, retaining some twenty bushels which had been rendered unsaleable by the presence of a weed known as "cheat", and which he intended to feed to the pigs. Settling their meal account they each bought a pair of shoes for ten bushels while John also acquired a plough and a couple of milk bowls for a further twenty bushels, and Rebecca coffee and meal. She had however to abandon her plan to buy some much needed material when she discovered that the price of only one yard of calico was either half a dollar or a bushel of wheat.

The arrival of the summer months revealed some of the beauties of Illinois. On the nearby prairie land, before the giant bluestem grass grew high enough to conceal both men and beasts, the ground was dotted with a myriad of wild flowers; cowslips, yellow and blue violets, ox eye daisies, sweet williams, roses, larkspur, dandelions and the dainty purple pasque flowers. On the wooded land ash, elm, walnut, cherry and mulberry trees also flourished, while plums, grapes, strawberries and raspberries grew wild in such abundance that they defeated even the preserving capacity of the diligent and thrifty Rebecca.

The Burland Farm at Barwick-in-Elmet.

The Old School House, Thorner.

John Burland.

Rebecca Burland.

Edward Burland, eldest son of John and Rebecca.

Mary Burland Yelliott, eldest daughter of John and Rebecca

Hannah Burland Dalby.

Charlotte Burland Burns.

Sarah Burland Allen.

William Burland.

George Bickerdike's cabin from a photograph taken in 1937.

John Bickerdike.

Hannah Briggs Bickerdike.

*Elizabeth Bickerdike Burland
1828-1910, who married
William Burland.*

Melons, pumpkins, cucumbers and peaches all ripened early and were a most welcome addition to the hitherto dreary diet of the pioneers. The children, running barefoot through the woods, collected piles of hickory and hazelnuts as well as filberts and walnuts, and these were spread out to dry and stored for the winter. Both in the clearing around their cabin and in the woods generally there was a far greater variety of birds, many of them much more colourful, than they had been used to in England. The red-throated humming birds with their ability to hover and fly backwards were particularly intriguing, while Rebecca was also fascinated by the many warblers, black and yellow orioles, scarlet tanagers and pretty bluebirds all so exotic in appearance that she believed them to be parrots. None however, not even the aptly named whippoorwill, whose haunting notes could be heard during the warm nights, was ever to compensate for the absence of either a robin or of a cuckoo, that most nostalgic of all English summer birds. In the bright sunlight butterflies, more brightly coloured than any she had seen before, settled outside the cabin door, drawn to a patch of ground where she tipped soapy water, and occasionally the family also spotted mink and opossum on their land. Sometimes however the wildlife proved to be more than a little alarming. On one occasion they discovered a set of footprints so like those of a small child that John, convinced that he was on the trail of either a fairy or an Indian child, followed them across a ploughed field. Needless to say he found no one and it was a long time before their neighbours were able to convince them that the prints had merely been those of a raccoon.

In early October John continued to bring more of their land under cultivation while he waited for the Indian corn, so laboriously sown, to mature. With its straight head-high stems, each bearing a drooping tassel of corn, and narrow, wavy leaves, it was surprisingly different in appearance from that they had known in England. Sadly however their first crop was a disappointment. Sown late and cultivated inefficiently, most of it failed to ripen, but it was nevertheless cut and stacked to be used later for seed. Although John knew that he should now be sowing his wheat for the following year, he had spent their few remaining dollars on a pig and therefore could not afford a team for the new plough. Accordingly he approached Mr. Knowles, a local farmer known to plough for hire, who refused a fifth of their produce from the eight acres in return for tilling the land, offering instead to do their ploughing in return for John's watch which had been purchased in England for less than a sovereign. John accepted this proposal with alacrity, and because the family had eaten no meat for some weeks other than a few chickens which Rebecca had acquired in return for a china tea cup, he also took the opportunity to acquire some young pigs at a dollar each. These they fed on the unsaleable wheat to improve the quality of the bacon, and within a month they had fattened so well that between them they provided some thirty stones of pork. Coupled with the plentiful harvest from their potato patch, this meant that the family was for once able to enjoy a rare period of comparatively luxurious living.

The first Sunday in November was the first anniversary of their arrival in America and an occasion to reflect a little on their achievements. Despite all their difficulties they now had four acres of wheat more than in their first season and owned their own plough even though they were still without a team. Their livestock had increased in value, and a further healthy calf had been born. Moreover a totally unexpected bonus was that Rebecca's health had improved enormously. Ever since she had exchanged the moist atmosphere of England for the dry climate of Illinois with its excessively cold winters and long hot summers, the asthma which had afflicted her since childhood had vanished completely. Setting aside this progress however, they were aware that they were at the start of yet another winter, and that the children were badly in need of new clothing which their parents still could not afford. Fortunately the family was amazingly tough and despite the deficiencies in their diet and their general lifestyle, they usually suffered little in the way of illness. On at least one occasion however they did succumb to an attack of fever, probably malarial, which John and Rebecca called "the ague". Malaria was endemic in Illinois in the early 1800's,[35] the risk of infection being especially high during the summer and autumn when whole families would fall victim to an attack on consecutive days. Although Rebecca put their own recovery down to the weak infusions of herbs which she administered, it was in fact probably spontaneous. No effective treatment was available and in any case in the pioneer lands doctors were unknown.

Their second winter was at first largely uneventful but Rebecca often became depressed during these cold and seemingly interminable cheerless days. Until new clothes could be acquired their attendance at prayer meetings was still out of the question and letters from home, in any case a highly unsatisfactory substitute for the friendship and family life they had formerly enjoyed, were so infrequent as to be almost non-existent. To make matters worse the date of their first anniversary had coincided with the celebrations of the annual feast in Barwick village, the memory of which made them all acutely homesick, and if it had been in any way possible they would have packed up there and then and returned. Unfortunately however no amount of wishing could alter the permanence of their position and in preparation for the onset of winter, John carried out some repairs and alterations to their cabin to try to make conditions a little more tolerable than they had been the previous year. With memories of that time and its constant demand for kindling still fresh in their minds, he and young John also stockpiled a massive quantity of logs which they hoped would be sufficient to last until the spring.

Shortly before Christmas they had a visit from Garret Van Dusen. He was a familiar figure in the district, a successful farmer and stock-trader hailing originally from Kentucky, but now a Commissioner of Pike County and responsible for establishing the ferry owned by the Phillips family. The purpose of his visit was to offer them a couple of young steers and a milk cow, an offer John found tempting because he was keen to increase the size of his herd as soon as possible. Sadly a lack of funds, together with only sufficient winter fodder to feed the stock he had already, meant that he had no choice but to refuse. Van Dusen however waved aside these difficulties suggesting that payment could be made when it was convenient. Although the interest rate at 25% was high, John nevertheless found the idea attractive as indeed did George with whom he discussed the proposition. On the strength of this John decided to go ahead giving van Dusen a promissory note for the $30 agreed, and arranging to pay the interest in due course, hoping meanwhile that their fodder could somehow be made to stretch through to the next season.

Towards the end of their second winter with feed running dangerously low and the appearance of the cattle impoverished, John eagerly anticipated the arrival of the new grass which he knew would swiftly improve their condition. However at the beginning of March, just as he was about to embark on his second sugar harvest, he was surprised to see Van Dusen appear unexpectedly, and displeased to find that the purpose of his visit was to make a peremptory demand for payment in full. Indignantly John protested the terms of their original deal which was that no time limit would be set, but Van Dusen's response was that it was exactly because the promissory note specified no time limit that he now wished to claim his money. Impervious to John's pleas for more time, Van Dusen threatened him with legal action and indeed the very next day a legal officer called to serve the Burlands with a writ permitting them only a few days in which to find the necessary funds. John and Rebecca were thus placed in an impossible position. There was no hope that they would be able to raise the money from their meagre resources, and they were only too well aware that if the cattle went to auction now their condition was certain to ensure a poor price. The land would then have to be sold up in order to pay off their debts and they would lose everything for which they had worked, a fact which had no doubt occurred to Van Dusen himself who had perhaps even engineered such a situation in the hope of getting his hands on their land. With great reluctance John therefore decided that they had no option but to solicit the help of George Bickerdike, asking either if he would be willing to make them a loan or to take some of the stock off their hands. After all it had been he who had initially commended the scheme to John.

The previous year had been a financially successful one for George. A combination of the frugal lifestyle which John and Rebecca had witnessed for themselves, hard work and wise expenditure had resulted in some good land supporting a large herd of healthy cattle, and his ambition now was to continue to prosper in the hope that one day he would be fortunate enough to have a son to whom he could leave a sizeable and profitable estate. Unfortunately for John and Rebecca however, this newly acquired prosperity did not mean that he was predisposed to show generosity towards his neighbours. As he pointed out while refusing to take any of the offending beasts off John's hands, he had no need of any further cattle at that time. Furthermore, on the subject of a loan he was similarly unhelpful, remaining unmoved by John's offer of generous interest repayments. It seemed that not even a reminder that without his enthusiastic recommendation the deal would never have been struck in the first place could bring about a change of heart.

John and Rebecca spent a sleepless night condemning both Van Dusen's sharp practice and their own negligence. They were also disheartened and disillusioned by the attitude of their fellow countryman whose behaviour seemed almost to amount to a betrayal, and which served to undermine their normally unshakeable belief in the bonds of friendship; Rebecca indeed was even temporarily deserted by her faith in the power of Providence. In the morning they rose feeling dispirited and no nearer any kind of solution. While John went through the motions of attending to the stock, Rebecca prepared breakfast which the children, sensing the mood of their parents, ate in silence. Half way through their meal they were interrupted by a knock at the door which John opened apprehensively, half expecting to find the bailiffs already outside. Instead on the threshold stood a somewhat sheepish George clutching a bundle of dollar bills. Apparently his lack of charity on the previous day had also caused him a sleepless night, and with the arrival of first light he had decided to loose no time in putting matters right. Privately Rebecca would not have been surprised to learn that this abrupt change of heart was the result of Ann's intervention, but whatever the influence her gratitude was heartfelt, and she soon forgave his initially tardy response. John, equally overwhelmed with relief was thus able to pay a surprised Van Dusen in full without further delay, and with the whole sorry affair at an end, and disaster narrowly averted, they turned their attention back to the land, wiser and with renewed vigour.

The two milk cows, two steers, heifer and calf, having been branded, were turned out and prospered on the new grass. They also had a good mare, and in addition the sugar harvest was even better than the previous one yielding 350 lbs., 40 lbs. of which was exchanged for a sow and a litter of pigs. Rebecca was also at last able to buy some material with which to make clothes, and they were still able to repay fifteen of the thirty dollars they had borrowed. To pay off the remainder of his debt, John had contracted to work for George on five days of the year, although he hoped that he would not be required too soon, for the time for sowing Indian corn was once more upon them and their own ploughing difficulties were still unresolved.

This lack of a team was a problem John had previously mentioned in passing to another near neighbour, a Mr. Burns. Now to their astonishment, aware that the time for ploughing was upon them, he arrived unbidden early one morning to turn over their land with his own team, and moreover with no thought of repayment. The Burlands were understandably delighted by this spontaneous gesture and the bonds of friendship between the two families, hitherto tenuous, strengthened as a result. It was comforting to feel that they had made some good friends and Rebecca began to feel that they were perhaps on their way to a better life at last. Certainly when she surveyed their property through the cabin door the sight was very gratifying. Although most of their land was as yet unbroken, a great deal of it had been cleared of timber, the fence around the new field was finished, and they had at least twelve acres under cultivation, eight with wheat and four with corn. There was even at last a little time now to spend on all those less important jobs which had been shelved until the crops were on their way. John dug over a rood of land, fencing it off so that Rebecca could start the small garden she had always wanted, and here she planted as many kinds of herbs as she could find, together with some of the vegetables and seeds donated by other, longer established, settlers. Most of these they had met at the prayer meetings, their attendance having been made possible by the arrival of summer weather and their recently acquired clothing.

By the end of June the wheat harvest was ready, a task for which John much preferred to use the old scythe which he had brought with him from England although its bluntness made reaping even harder work than usual, and caused him to yearn for a piece of good Yorkshire sharpening stone. While he struggled to mow the now luxuriant crop, Rebecca, as she had done the year previously, left the children in the care of Hannah, and took John junior with her to the fields where they both worked alongside her husband using the sickles provided by George. The three of them cutting at the rate of an acre a day had almost finished when George infuriatingly decided to lay claim to John's promised days of labour. Although it was not the most convenient time for him to be away from their own land, they were considerably indebted to their neighbour. Consequently Rebecca and her son found themselves on their own at yet another harvest time.

The work was as hard and the heat as oppressive as before but unlike the previous year Rebecca now had the added burden of being six months pregnant. Several times during the day, exhaustion compelled her to rest on a pile of sheaves where, puzzled by a peculiar buzzing sound, she was horrified to find a fully grown rattlesnake. Without pausing for thought and seizing the nearest implement, she belaboured the snake vigorously about the head until such time as she could be sure it was dead. A second, also lurking nearby, was similarly despatched. Perhaps not surprisingly this shock rendered her so weak that for a time she was unable to carry on with her work. In the evening the children triumphantly carried home the dead snake to show to their father who was suitably impressed by his wife's courage. The bite of the rattlesnake was swiftly fatal if no antidote was administered. A neighbour of the Burlands, bitten in the foot, had hurried to the nearest house for assistance but although the distance was not great, he had been obliged to call out the nature of his complaint as he approached, fearing that his tongue and limbs, already severely affected by paralysis would have become useless by the time he arrived. He subsequently made a full recovery but he had been unconscious before the antidote could be administered. From then on no matter how tired she became Rebecca was very careful where she sat. In fact, while working on the land she found it wise to take precautions before sitting anywhere for the insects in Illinois also posed something of a threat. All were considerably larger than those with which she had been familiar in England, ants in particular being half the size of the honey bee.

In all it took Rebecca and young John two days to finish the reaping and the day following John returned to their land. By noon they had bound the remainder of the wheat leaving the children to collect and stack the sheaves and while Rebecca prepared a mid-day meal, John took little Sarah over to the new fields to see the fires which he had kindled. When land was reclaimed from the forest, the trees were not felled at ground level but were left to dry out in the hot sun before being burned away later. Fascinated by the fire, and while her father's attention was momentarily distracted, Sarah unfortunately got too near to the leaping flames, her dress igniting quickly. Before John was able to catch her, the screaming child, rushing wildly round and round the field, had kindled all the sheaves and by the time John had pursued and caught her, smothered the burning clothes, and assured himself that she was not seriously hurt, their precious wheat was well alight and burning fiercely. Grabbing whatever utensil was to hand, the entire family, including the pregnant Rebecca who had rushed outside in response to her daughter's screams and her husband's shouts, ran too and fro between the stream and their crops in an attempt to extinguish the flames. Clearly it was a forlorn task. The straw was tinder dry and the heat of the blaze, coupled with the heat of the sun, made conditions unbearable for the fire-fighters. Eventually it was obvious that the unaffected sheaves would have to be isolated at the side of the field untouched by the flames, thereby allowing the inferno to run its course with the remainder. Thus, although they lost about an acre of wheat, they succeeded in saving seven. More important however was the fact that Sarah had miraculously come through her ordeal completely unharmed, and certainly in better shape than her mother. The events of this harvest had taken its toll of each of them but no one had suffered more than she, advanced in pregnancy but still doing the work of a man in the fields and a woman in the home. This latest crisis over, she sat in her rocking chair weeping from the combined effects of shock and exhaustion.

Where the fire had raged there was now a vista of charred and blackened land but fortunately they were able to turn this to their advantage, paying Knowles three dollars to plough for them and sowing it with a crop of turnips. This arrangement with Knowles turned out to be money well spent for breaking up virgin land was a difficult job requiring a huge plough and a large team. Of all the tasks on the farm, ploughing, by far the most important, was the one to cause them the greatest concern, and when John was eventually given lessons by their friend, Burns, in the art of yoking and driving his own team, his sense of achievement was immense.

On the whole the wheat they had saved was good although out of two hundred and twenty bushels about forty were unsaleable due to the presence of cheat. This grain bought more clothing for the family, paid off their account for salt which was so necessary for the quality of the milk, and provided harness for the oxen which they had bought from Garret Van Dusen and with which they proposed to plough their reclaimed land in the autumn. After this spree forty dollars remained, an unusual state of affairs in the Burland economy, and it was decided to leave it gathering interest in the hands of Mr. Varley in readiness for a rainy day. For the first time since their arrival they felt they were on their way to full independence at last.

CHAPTER IX

Deaths and Difficulties

IN THE AUTUMN of 1833 with the first frosts fingering the leaves, Rebecca gave birth to stillborn twins. The outcome of this pregnancy was hardly surprising in view of what she had endured during the preceding months coupled with the fact that she was now in her forty first year. Of the fourteen children she had conceived, only half had survived, five dying at, or shortly after, birth, and a further two in infancy. The latest babies were buried in the forest by John, and Rebecca was left physically weak and low in spirits although life was not all bleak. She was still able to take some pleasure from the garden John had made, now providing them with potatoes, carrots, turnips, onions, cabbages and pumpkins, and they also grew a small amount of tobacco for their own use. Nancy Phillips had of course been an inveterate smoker, and when once she had overcome her initial prejudice, Rebecca also found that she too enjoyed her own regular pipe. She also enjoyed accompanying her children on walks in the woods on summer evenings where they found many of the herbs familiar from home. Balm, horehound, penny royal, fennel, coriander and sage were all plentiful, although the latter was quite different from the variety they had known in England; mint was scarce, thyme apparently unobtainable. All the culinary or medicinal herbs hung in bunches from the roof of the cabin alongside joints of salted venison and pork for the coming winter months, and prior to her confinement, Rebecca had also laid down a quantity of butter. Undoubtedly they had much for which to be thankful. From other families who had recently settled nearby they frequently heard unsettling accounts of bad voyages, extreme poverty, sickness and death which made their own misfortunes often seem slight. Also some of their hard work was now beginning to pay dividends and even if the returns were only small, they had so far at least managed to keep their heads above water. Moreover as the number of settlers in the area increased, so more amenities became available.

Especially welcome was a new preaching centre in the home of George Lytle. Hitherto prayer meetings had involved a long walk which was taxing for the younger children. These new meetings were organised by the Atlas Mission under the stewardship of Peter Cartwright who was renowned for his outspoken sermons, and the Burlands were filled with eager anticipation. Sadly this all too quickly turned to disappointment for while Cartwright undoubtedly filled a very real need for some people, such fundamental and unstructured worship could not have been further removed from the formality and restraint which was John and Rebecca's own concept of religion. Whipped up into a state bordering on frenzy, the congregation sang, shouted and swooned, joined hands and danced, knelt and shuddered in trance-like states uttering ecstatic cries, tore their hair and convulsed upon the ground supposedly in the grip of some omnipotent power. Although in the absence of any alternative, the family persevered in their attendance for some time, it was not long before they ceased to attend altogether.

Autumn, or the fall as they soon learned to call it, was an exceptionally pretty time of the year, the colours of the foliage being so much more florid and dramatic than the muted tints of home. Sitting in her rocking chair in the cabin doorway Rebecca was fascinated by the riot of colour in the surrounding woodlands, the vivid golds and yellows, bronzes and scarlets of the hickory, oak and maple trees, and the clustered crimson berries of the sumacs. In October John sowed yet another crop of wheat. The acquisition of their own ploughing facilities meant that this task was now both more pleasurable and much quicker. Afterwards he continued to clear as much of their remaining land as possible. It was important to press on with this work for there was so much available and the sooner it was bought and broken, the sooner it could be made profitable. The following winter was fortunately uneventful, and in the spring the cattle were released into the woods as usual and the corn sown. Unfortunately however, the sugar crop was not nearly as good as on previous occasions although it did provide them with sufficient funds to repay the last of their debt to George.

In June they learned of an opportunity to expand even further. Their neighbour, Mr. Paddock, having obtained his land on pre-emption, had now decided to sell his improvement right. Not renowned for his addiction to hard work, over the last three years he had made little headway, and for the fifteen acres he had managed to clear, he offered John first refusal in return for fifty dollars which he was prepared to accept in the form of cattle and wheat. A further incentive

70

was his house, the condition of which was reasonably good. John's experience with Van Dusen had made a careful man even more cautious. Although he was sorely tempted by the offer, it would mean sinking everything they possessed into the venture. Paddock would take some of their stock but within a year payment would have to be made in full to the land office where the claim was registered. On the other hand they were very eager to expand, the land in question adjoined their property and the asking price was a fair one. Eventually, after much deliberation, John and Rebecca decided that they would be foolish to miss the opportunity. If at the end of the year they still found themselves unable to pay for the title deeds, then they would have forfeited some wheat and stock but should be in a position to withstand such a loss without too much hardship. Paddock was accordingly given a cow and a heifer together with seventy bushels of wheat, in return supplying John with a pre-emption certificate endorsed with his name. Shortly afterwards he left the district to become established on another plot before the winter.

Once he had left the family lost no time in hastening over to inspect their new territory. They had already decided to remain in their old home and to use Paddock's cabin for storage purposes. Now they planned how best to utilise the new land. Before they were able to go ahead however, John was approached by a stranger introducing himself as Mr. Carr, who asked several pertinent questions concerning the pre-emption right of Paddock's land. Fearing that their caller might be considering taking possession of the empty house, John was careful to concede as little information as possible. Prior to 1841 the pre-emption system was open to all manner of abuse, and was unable to provide the settler with any real security. Conflict between squatters and those who held legal title was common, and John knew that he would have no real peace of mind until the land office had been paid in full and the title deeds were irrefutably his. Unfortunately however, because he was relying on his sugar profits for the necessary capital, it would be spring before these were available, and in the meantime Carr and his family must be prevented from occupying the property at all costs.

Although the Burland's initial response to Carr's visit was that the cabin should be burned down rather than that he should be allowed to take it over, their subsequent determination to use it for storage left them with only one alternative. One of them would have to move in to take possession, and as John was fully occupied with the care of their stock, that caretaker would inevitably have to be Rebecca.

71

Understandably this prospect evoked little enthusiasm. Not only did she dislike the idea of leaving John, she was more than a little apprehensive at the possibility of having to repel interlopers. On the other hand she was fiercely determined to prevent Carr from cheating them out of their property, and as she considered herself well used to coping with isolation this was neither the time nor the place to become faint hearted. Within the day she had moved into Paddock's old home taking with her Sarah and William, a bed, some food and a few essential cooking utensils.

At first the weeks passed uneventfully although she found the nights long, lonely and frightening. The days were more tolerable because John and the other children were scarcely half a mile away and she had just begun to believe that all would be well when one afternoon she heard the rumble of an approaching waggon carrying Carr accompanied by a woman and two small children, together with a large quantity of furniture. Only too aware of their intentions Rebecca hastily slammed the door and attempted to tie up the latch, but Carr was not to be deterred. Forcing his way into the cabin, he proceeded to show his family around with a sublime disregard for her presence and protestations, and even began to instal their own furniture. Eventually he informed Rebecca that as her company was unwelcome, she had better return to her own home immediately. Such effrontery greatly intensified Rebecca's determination. If Carr had expected her to turn tail and return to John, he had sorely underestimated her spirit for the thought of accepting defeat never occurred to her. Instead she merely moved herself and her children together with their bed into the other room of the cabin, and set about awaiting the arrival of her husband.

It was evening before John arrived forcing his way into the cabin to discover his wife and children prisoners on their own property. Once assured of their safety he angrily demanded the immediate departure of the squatters, but when confronted Carr defiantly produced a certificate purporting to be the legal title to the estate which he claimed had been issued by the land office in Quincy. John knew that Carr could not have purchased the land legally. Either he was bluffing and had been nowhere near the land office, or he had fraudulently sworn an oath that the land was still in its virgin state and not in the process of being improved by someone else. Conferring briefly he and Rebecca therefore concluded that the situation could only be resolved by John himself taking the relevant documents to Quincy so that judgement could be pronounced. By this time, Carr, enraged by their whispering, had decided to leave the cabin, declaring truculently that since they appeared to be intent on occupying his house, he in his turn would occupy theirs, and it was indeed there that John later discovered him. Pausing only to evict the unwelcome guests, and arranging for the other children and the stock to be cared for by the Burns family. The next morning he delivered a supply of food to Rebecca and began the ride to Quincy.

John was away for three days which seemed an eternity to Rebecca who found herself in a quite farcical position. She and her two children were virtual prisoners, confined to one room which they dared not leave, while Carr, taking full advantage of John's absence, subjected them to constant harassment including casting doubt on the likelihood of their ever seeing John again. In these efforts he was joined by several friends who called round and were equally abusive and threatening. These so-called friends may have been members of a claim club which were formed by squatters to assist settlers in the acquisition of land. Their members were opposed to expansion by established farmers which they felt prevented the new settler from gaining a foothold, and they were especially assiduous in their efforts when, as in this instance, the dispute was over the more valuable timbered land.[36]

The only person to show the family some compassion was Mrs. Carr who occasionally openly chided her husband for his cruel remarks although her efforts were largely ineffective. However, Rebecca found that she was at least able to take some comfort from them, as indeed she also did from her Bible. Indeed the sight of her calmly reading aloud from it to her children so infuriated Carr that he declared that he would get rid of her and her 'accursed religion' for good.

On the third day of her captivity, Rebecca was much encouraged to receive a visit from a group of her own friends and neighbours who had been made aware of her plight by the Burns family. Refused admission, the women contrived to communicate with the prisoners through a gap in the wall, while the men in the party threatened to overwhelm their captors. Carr soon found that he had no choice but to open the door, allowing Rebecca's supporters to flock in and pack the cabin, but when they seized upon her Bible and began to hold their customary evening service, it was more than he could tolerate. In a fury he and his family withdrew from the premises so that John, returning later the same night, found Rebecca celebrating victory in the midst of friends.

The trip to Quincy had proved John's suspicions beyond all doubt. Although he had paid in full for the title deeds, Carr had indeed omitted to declare any improvements, a fraudulent declaration which rendered him liable to a substantial fine. For Rebecca the best news of all was that at last she and the children could return to their own home where next morning they received a visit from a contrite Mrs. Carr. Her husband, it appeared, was now willing to compromise, an abrupt change of heart which had no doubt been inspired by the realisation that as a result of his double-dealing he found himself in an absurd predicament. Either he would have to pay the Burlands for the pre-emption certificate on the property, or he would have to sell them the title deeds for which he had already paid in full. John despised the man both for his treatment of Rebecca and for the despicable way in which he now sheltered behind his wife, but despite having little taste for such a neighbour, he too was in an awkward situation. One certificate was no good without the other, and he still had insufficient capital to pay for the title deeds. Therefore, summoning his opponent in person, he offered him possession of the land in return for a sum of eighty dollars, terms more generous than Carr deserved, and which needless to say he readily accepted. John meanwhile, despite having lost the opportunity of expanding his own holding for the time being, was at least thirty dollars better off.

John and Rebecca also had difficulty with the law on other occasions. Having bought land it was important for a settler to find out if it possessed a water mill. If so, the wisest precaution was for him to have it condemned, a move which ensured that no one else could build a mill within two miles of his own site, and assured its owner of a monopoly if he should wish to build a mill for himself in the future. If he ultimately decided against building, he was then in possession of a valuable site which he would be able to sell off. Settlers were permitted two years in which to determine the course they wished to adopt. If at the end of that period they had not come to a decision, they forfeited both the site and any money which they might have gained from the sale. Soon after their arrival John and Rebecca discovered such a site on their land and as a result of George's advice, had it condemned with a view to selling later. Some eighteen months afterwards Andrew Phillips offered to buy from them, accepting John's asking price of $150, but as the money was not readily available, it was arranged that Phillips should pay for it at a more convenient time. An attempt by John to draw up an official agreement was greeted with scorn by Phillips who was at pains to assure him that his word was his bond which unfortunately proved not to be the case. On various pretexts Phillips continued to avoid payment until the two years had elapsed, at which time Phillips own employer erected a mill near the Burland property. Thus John and Rebecca were doubly cheated, losing the opportunity of becoming millers in their own right, and failing to profit from the sale of a suitable site. The land laws of their new country, framed hastily and administered inefficiently, caused many such disputes and difficulties for the new settler.

The dispute with Carr finally settled, John turned his attention back to the land. John junior was now twelve and already capable of doing a full days work on the farm. This allowed Rebecca to devote more of her time to household tasks but first Hannah and then Charlotte also took their share of that work, and she therefore found herself in the unusual situation of being able to sit back a little and enjoy the fruits of their labours. The following three or four years were highly productive. They now owned seven horses including some foals, their herd of cattle had gradually increased to twenty, providing them with an ample quantity of milk and beef, and besides the usual pigs, there were also a few sheep and some poultry. Nor was the house itself short of improvement. All their early home-made furniture and utensils had been discarded in favour of items bought at the local store, and they had built up a more than adequate supply of bed linen and clothing. In addition, a new cabin was planned for which John had earmarked a suitable and more open situation a short distance away. Now it was just a matter of clearing more land and he and young John would be able to spend their quieter moments working on it. Rebecca could scarcely believe the improvement in their circumstances, and it was a source of continual wonderment and delight that they owned everything and rented nothing.

Nor was isolation the problem it had once been. Each year more families settled in the vicinity so that small townships now surrounded them. The town of Griggsville was founded in 1833, and most of the dense forest that had greeted them had already fallen to the pioneer's axe so that new paths and cart-tracks now crossed the land between the homesteads. They and their children enjoyed meeting these newcomers who brought with them that sense of kinship and security which Rebecca had so missed in the early days. As the struggle for survival during those years had abated, they had found time to play their own part in building up the little community, regularly attending a Methodist society at Detroit three miles away. Rebecca was undaunted by the wolves she sometimes encountered in the woods during the six mile round trip, a trek she made barefoot in order to preserve her shoes, slipping them on only as she neared her destination. In 1841 another group was formed at nearby Griggsville, of which Nancy Phillips and Ann Bickerdike were early members, and the Burlands left the Detroit branch to unite with them. Meetings were held in the home of another Boone descendant, before a preacher who rejoiced in the name of Moses Clampit. Later the members gathered at the home of one Richard Wade, and it was here that they at last decided to build a church. The men of the community did the work themselves on land donated by Richard, and within two months the frame, thirty feet wide and thirty six feet long, had been built. In December 1843 this building, named Bethel, was dedicated, an achievement which seemed to set the seal of permanence on their venture. In 1844 the land around the church became a regular burial ground, but as early as 1840 or 1841 there had already been one interment, a child of the Lytle family believed to have been badly mauled while riding in the forest, reputedly by a panther, and buried in an unmarked grave in much the same way as John had buried their own twin babies.

While John and Rebecca's own fortunes were prospering, George Bickerdike's financial affairs were also going from strength to strength. His policy of working hard and spending little had paid handsome dividends. As well as owning some four hundred acres of land, he now possessed a large herd of cattle and the considerable sum of money he had amassed had enabled him to make several loans on which he received generous interest repayments. Sadly however, six years of marriage had failed to result in the birth of any children. He and his wife Ann were frequent visitors to the Burlands, but one September day in 1838 he called on his own, chiefly to visit Rebecca who had been unwell for some time. Afterwards John, and John junior, now aged sixteen, proudly took their visitor to view their rapidly expanding holding, sharing with him their hopes for the future. Unfortunately for George there was to be no such future. Within only a few hours he had developed the symptoms of typhoid fever, dying a couple of days later.

Rebecca, anxious to help, wrote home to Edward asking him to call and personally break the news to George's brother, John, still living on the home farm in Thorner. Unlike his hitherto more fortunate brother, John had a large family to support, including several sons, and although agriculture in England was no longer in the parlous state of earlier years, he was still only a tenant farmer on the estate of the Earl of Mexborough, and likely to remain so. It was thus only natural that the news of his wealthy brother's death should be received with interest as well as sorrow. Over the years George's letters had charted his progress to the delight and not a little envy of his siblings. John calculated that by now his brother's estate must be substantial and awaited further events with eagerness. In fact George had died intestate. Of the land he left, Ann retained one hundred and forty acres which she proposed to farm on her own account, while the remainder was divided between John and his sisters, Bessie and Dinah.

John and his wife agonised for a long time over whether to claim their inheritance. Bessie and Dinah, married and well settled in England, had no desire to take up their own legacies, and were quite willing to sell their shares to their only remaining brother. Eventually John decided to investigate the situation for himself and in 1842, in the company of a friend who for a long time had also had a fancy to try his luck abroad, he boarded ship and sailed for America. Neither Ann Bickerdike nor the Burlands had any indication of John's impending arrival, and Rebecca was therefore both astonished and delighted when she discovered that the man on their land one morning, bearing a remarkable resemblance to their late neighbour, was in fact his brother. In their recently completed cabin, so vastly superior to the previous one, John and Rebecca gladly offered the men hospitality, and during the whole of that evening questioned them avidly for news of family and friends and the place that, despite all their success, they still regarded as home. Before they left next day John showed the visitors around his land. They could not have failed to be impressed. The original eighty acres had now swelled to some three hundred and sixty, half of which was already under cultivation, highly productive and supporting two tenant farmers paying John a rent of a dollar an acre.

Some of their progress at least was undoubtedly due to the fact that since the age of fourteen, John junior had been doing the work of a man. Without a son their profits would have been considerably less for they would have had to pay a hired hand about ten dollars a month. It is doubtful if John was paid any wage at all. Most sons of the early pioneers worked only for their keep, although in return they did receive some assistance from their parents when the time came for them to set up on their own account. Over the years some men contrived to build up considerable acreages with a view to the time when their sons would marry, and many a young couple received a valuable wedding present of land, a system which not only preserved family unity but ensured that elderly farmers were not burdened with more land than they could comfortably manage at the end of their working lives.

The following day John Bickerdike's travelling companion succeeded in finding employment locally as a day labourer at a wage of fourteen dollars a month inclusive of full board. John meanwhile, having inspected his brother's fertile land, had no more doubts where his own destiny lay. It would however be necessary for him to return to England to dispose of the farm in Thorner, and to make arrangements for the transportation of his family. At the mention of England, Rebecca was overcome with nostalgia. For years she had dreamed of the place she still thought of as home and she longed to see her two eldest children again. Edward, now married, had only recently established himself in his own school, and Mary, also married, now had a family of her own. If Rebecca was ever to undertake the arduous journey she felt it had to be now, and the opportunity of an escort was too good to be missed. Despite the fact that many of her friends thought her too old to make such a long voyage and her children repeatedly begged her to remain, in April 1842, leaving the household in the capable hands of Hannah, now nineteen, and sixteen year old Charlotte, she and John Bickerdike travelled by steamboat up the Ohio River and on through Cincinatti and Philadelphia to New York. Two months later, on the 19th June, they arrived safely in the old country, eleven eventful years since Rebecca had leaned out over the rail of the "Home" to say goodbye.

CHAPTER X

The Last Return

REBECCA'S VISIT WAS a huge success. Although her parents were now dead, she was able to visit her brothers and sisters as well as old friends in Horsforth and Barwick. Everyone was eager for a first hand account of her experiences, and because she herself had suffered from over-glorified accounts of American life, she was careful not to gloss over the many hardships the family had endured. To this end her own account was diligently recorded by her eldest son. The reunion with her two eldest children was undoubtedly the highlight of her visit. At first she and Edward scarcely recognised each other, and Rebecca was so overcome that the meeting almost proved too much for her. Sadly attempts to persuade him to return with her were unsuccessful, Edward fearing that his weak lungs might suffer from the effects of a prolonged journey by sea and the difference in climate although in fact they may well have benefited from such a change. One consolation however was the decision of her daughter, Mary, and her son-in-law, Luke Yelliott to accompany her with their two children. In addition they were also joined by several friends from Barwick and Thorner who planned to settle in John and Rebecca's neighbourhood. The party sailed from Liverpool in the middle of September, and this time Rebecca must have known that the break was final. She never again returned to her home country, and mother and son were never to meet again.

On his return to England, John Bickerdike arranged for the transfer of Carr Farm at Thorner to his wife's brother-in-law, William Leatham, giving each of his sisters £25 for their share of the American land. By 1843 he and his wife, Hannah, their sons, James, George, John, Richard, William and Charles, their daughters, Elizabeth and Mary, a niece, Christiana Hargrave, and a nephew, Thomas Dalby, were ready to sail from Liverpool. Eight weeks under sail left two lasting memories in the minds of the children. A baby daughter born to John and Hannah during the voyage, failed to survive and was buried at sea, while young James, the eldest boy, never forgot the one and only toy he had taken with him, a spinning top which was ruthlessly thrown overboard by the master of the ship with the excuse that it might damage the wood of the deck. Once in New York, John hired a man with a team of four horses to transport his family and their luggage overland. However the party was so large that it proved impossible to fit them all into the waggon at the same time, and they therefore took turns to walk alongside until they arrived in Pekin, Illinois, a distance of some eight hundred miles. There, footsore and weary, they boarded a boat which took them along the Illinois River to Phillips Ferry.

The large Bickerdike clan was still incomplete for in 1843 a seventh son was born and baptised Robert. Four of John and Hannah's sons eventually served in the United States Army during the Civil War, the second, George, dying from bullet wounds received at the Battle of Holly Springs on December 30th, 1862. A memorial to him, and to another boy from Thorner, Edwin Nettleton, who died a year later at the Battle of Mission Ridge, stands in Bethel churchyard. John and Hannah Bickerdike were eventually to become the grandparents of forty two children, most of whom continued to live nearby and to share in the life of the new community. In 1856 their eldest daughter, Elizabeth, united the two old Thorner families by marrying William Burland, the baby Rebecca had carried all the way from Barwick to Illinois. Like all the Bickerdikes and Burlands, Elizabeth was a staunch member of the Methodist Episcopal Church and worked hard to support Bethel Church. Other relatives who settled a little further north at Griggsville helped to build and maintain a church there too, but in 1904 it was burned to the ground while Elizabeth watched, her eight year old grand-daughter Edith at her side. 'If God can't take care of his church, he can't take care of me,' sobbed the child. 'Maybe he has something better in mind', replied Elizabeth. The new church, more beautiful than the old, still stands in Griggsville and contains a stained glass window bearing the names of the donors, William and Elizabeth Burland. To the end of their long lives, William and Elizabeth were unswervingly loyal to the faith in which their own seven surviving children were reared. Both are buried in Bethel Cemetery. In 1883 the Rev. Thomas Weems who had recently been appointed to Bethel Church decided that his congregation was in need of a larger church, and accordingly the old church was moved to the opposite side of the road, the new church being built on the old site. Comprising two class rooms, a gallery and a vestibule, the cost, $3544, was borne by the community.

In 1949 Helen Birch Filson, the grand-daughter of William and Elizabeth, came to England from her home in Florida. The trip had been long awaited. Some years previously in a chest belonging to her grandmother, she had discovered a letter from the William Leatham who had taken over Carr Farm, evidently written in response to one from America for it began with the writer expressing his relief for the safe arrival of the addressee in Illinois. Discussing the financial affairs of the farm and detailing the yield of the previous year, William also mentioned the names of several of the fields, and because Mrs. Filson intended one day to visit Thorner, she retained the letter in the hope that these names would eventually lead her to the home of her ancestors. Arriving in the village, the driver of the taxi-cab which she had hired in Leeds, showed the letter to some of the residents who directed them to Carr Farm where the tenants, a Mr. and Mrs. Walmsley, were able to show Mrs. Filson their lease with its reference to Joseph Batty who had taken over the premises from William Leatham. They were also able to show her the fields which still bore the old names mentioned in the letter. Reared on her grandmother's stories of childhood, Mrs. Filson was overjoyed to find that so little had changed when Mrs. Walmsley escorted her round the house pointing out the stone staircase, flagged floors and old fireplaces. Elizabeth Bickerdike Burland had often talked of Old Nanny who lived in a one room cottage at the turn of the lane and the cottage was still there, as indeed was a pigeon cote referred to in William's letter.

Back in the village Mrs. Filson visited the old Methodist Chapel, the school room where Miss Frances Whincup had taught the Bickerdike children in the 1830's and early 1840's, and talked to several of the older villagers some of whom either remembered, or were related to, her ancestors. One astonished the visitor by producing a sampler done at the village school and signed Hannah Dalby, aged 13, 1825, identical to that worked by Elizabeth Bickerdike Burland which hung in her American home, and which had also been executed in Miss Whincup's school. Hannah Dalby, a member of a large family of that name, may have been related to the Thomas Dalby who emigrated with the Bickerdikes.

Before returning to Florida, Mrs. Filson also visited the house at Garforth where Edward Burland had taught, his home in Swillington where she was given a tour of the building by the occupants, and Barwick-in-Elmet, her grandfather's birthplace. She was however quite horrified by the 'wicked maypole' in the centre of the village, expressing the opinion that many a young 'swain and damsel must have gone to Hell for dancing round it'. Just as her ancestors had left England in the wake of the Napoleonic Wars, so Mrs. Filson found her visit affected by the aftermath of the Second World War. England was finding a return to normality hard. Food rationing was still in force and hospitality was therefore difficult. Of necessity her visit had to be short, and on her return home she expressed her regret in a letter to a relative which reveals more than a tinge of wistfulness. 'Maybe some-time I can go back and just browse around the little villages', she said, 'they were such quiet restful places, untouched by the hideousness of war and the noise and bustle of the commercial world'. Sadly to-day no one in the family knows if her wish was ever fulfilled.

Following the death of George Bickerdike on September 24th, 1838, his wife, Ann continued to live in their cabin and to farm the land with the assistance of her nephew, Alfred Andrew Elledge, the son of Ann's sister, Elizabeth and her husband, the preacher Jesse Elledge. Ann's efforts at farming were very creditable. The year fol-lowing George's death, she produced two hundred pounds of beef and one hundred and seventy pounds of bacon as well as butter and tallow, and also spun linsey on her own loom. She remained in the cabin con-tinuing to farm her hundred and forty acres until her death on the 22nd March, 1844. As for George's cabin which he had built himself in 1828, despite being the ramshackle edifice Rebecca first knew, it was still standing in 1937, one hundred and nine years later. Ann's brother, also Andrew, who had met John and Rebecca when they first stepped ashore in Pike County, died in 1864 at the age of 63 and was buried alongside his daughter Cenia, in Bethel Cemetery.

Edward Burland, the eldest son of John and Rebecca, spent the years following his retirement in Swillington, near Leeds. A much respected schoolmaster he was always to suffer from ill health, and this coupled with a studious nature encouraged him to turn to the writing of poetry for which he became well known locally. A volume of his poems entitled 'Village Rhymes; or Poems on various subjects princi-pally appertaining to incidents in village life' was published in 1858 while a novel, 'Amy Thornton', published by a Leeds firm, appeared in 1863. In 1855 he also published 'A Catechism of English History'. In 1839 when he was classical tutor at Hawkshaw School, a private boarding establishment for boys aged between eight and fourteen at West Garforth, near Leeds, Edward married and began a private school of his own in Hunslet, now part of the city of Leeds. He began by post-ing leaflets through the doors of local houses advertising the school but for three days no one turned up. However, on the fourth day, one very apprehensive girl arrived and by the following week, several more had been enrolled. Within six weeks his school was a paying concern, and continued to be so until 1857 when he retired. Edward, deeply impressed by his mother's stories, wrote an account of her experiences which was published after Rebecca's return to Illinois. He died at Swillington on the 6th April, 1875, three years after his wife, Hannah who was seven years his senior. They had no children, and the couple are buried together in the village churchyard, the inscription on his tombstone reading:

'In memory of Edward Burland of Swillington, schoolmaster, who died April 6th, 1875, aged 61 years. Under many social disabilities he acquired, and under extreme delicacy of constitution he taught with marked success, a competent knowledge of the classics, mathematics and other branches of science and literature. As an original thinker his prose works, and as an elegant writer, his poetry will long remain evidence of his powers and ability. Cautious, peaceful and retiring by nature, he lived respected and he died truly deserving the character of being a "just man".'

Edward left a comfortable sum of money to be divided between his five brothers and sisters, which each of them used to great advantage in the purchase of still more land. Today Edward's cottage still stands in a narrow lane on the edge of green fields.

Edward's sister Mary had married her husband Luke, a maltster, on the 3rd February, 1840 in the parish church of Sandal Magna, Wakefield, the scene of her mother's baptism forty three years earlier, and after the ceremony the couple set up home together at Westgate Common in Wakefield. In October of that year, Mary gave birth to healthy twin daughters, Sarah and Rebecca, but in September 1842 her six week old son Edward died from pneumonia, and it was perhaps this tragedy which prompted Mary and Luke to accompany Rebecca when she returned. The twins celebrated their second birthday on board ship, and a few months after their arrival in America Mary had a second set of twins, John and Annette. There were to be four more children, Luke junior, Edward, Mary and William. In Illinois, Luke senior earned his living as a butcher and farmer. Both he and Mary are buried in Griggsville.

Luke junior was born in 1845, the year in which the district got its first school. The schoolmaster was yet another Yorkshireman, William Turnbull, formerly a flax manufacturer in York, who held classes in his cabin during the winter months. Luke Yelliott junior lived and died on his parents farm near Detroit. Always known locally as "young Luke" he married Maria Davis and the couple subsequently had five children. Remembered with great affection he was a kindly, home-loving man, honest and hard-working, both on behalf of his own family and his local church where he was eventually buried. In 1942 over a hundred direct descendants of his parents, Luke and Mary, gathered together at Ocean Trail Park on the Illinois River. While seven members of the family were absent due to service in the armed forces, the remainder of the clan enjoyed fried chicken and an iced cake, decorated with the Stars and Stripes and presented to the gathering by a descendant, Leta Yelliott Whalen of Chicago. Afterwards the older members of the family were entertained by the younger.

John Burland, the daring boy who climbed out along the bowsprit of the 'Home' remained adventurous to the end. He died in 1847 at the early age of twenty six during an incident which occurred when he was returning home after seeing service with the Army in the Mexican War. The tragedy began innocently enough with John teasing one of his fellow soldiers by pouring sand into his soup. In the ensuing brawl John was killed, and after his body had been buried alongside the Santa Fe Trail, his comrades fired a salute over his grave. Hannah, the little girl on whom Rebecca had so often relied in the early days, subsequently married in 1849, Thomas Dalby, the nephew of the Bickerdikes who emigrated with them. They had only one daughter, Mary, after whose birth Hannah was confined to a wheelchair. She died in her ninetieth year, twelve years after her husband. Hannah's younger sister Charlotte, married in 1848 Daniel Burns, the son of the couple who were such staunch friends to John and Rebecca. Charlotte and Daniel had three daughters, Hannah, Sarah and Martha. One of Hannah's grandchildren, Floyd Phillips was himself to become another pioneer helping to open up the last great western frontier between America and Canada in the 1930's. It was Floyd's ultimate success in British Columbia which financed his three brothers and enabled them to farm their own land. The youngest Burland daughter, Sarah, whose burning clothing had ignited the harvest, married Francis Allen in 1852 and had three children, Francis, or Frank, Charlotte and David.

In later life John and Rebecca lived with Mary and Luke Yelliott while the land they had so carefully accumulated passed, as they had always wished, to their only surviving son, William. Rebecca relished those leisured years, surrounded by friends, neighbours, children and grandchildren who enjoyed her stories of a childhood in a strange land,

and of a voyage into a new world, and they recalled her smoking her pipe by the fireside and sitting in the rocking chair which she had taken with her from England. This chair which has travelled so far and seen so much is still in regular use, and now stands in the Illinois home of Leslie Allen, a direct descendant of Rebecca. In 1983 when Bethel Church celebrated its centenary it took pride of place while also on show were many antiques, quilts and pictures illustrating the history of the church and of those who have worshipped there over the years.

Sometime during the 1860's, Rebecca's brother, John Burton, visited his sister in Illinois and it was perhaps he who on his return reported to Edward that his parents were beginning to show signs of aging. On the 9th April, 1871 John Burland died aged 88. After almost sixty years of hardship and happiness, Rebecca was alone and the companionship and affection they had shared, was unable to survive separation. Nine months later, on the 31st January, 1872 at the age of 79, she joined her husband in Bethel Cemetery.

Many other Yorkshire families eventually followed the example of the Burlands. Among them were the Nettletons who had been scythe stone makers in Thorner, and the Briggs and the Dalby families together with the Robinsons and the Turnbulls, all solid and industrious West Riding farmers. The cemetery at Bethel Church testifies to the English influence in the neighbourhood, its headstones covered with names from the old country, Dixon, Rhodes, Moore, Lister, Biddle, Colman, Hill, Blezzard, Husband and many others.

Other settlers from Yorkshire had been well established American citizens when John and Rebecca arrived. Benjamin and Ann Butterfield for example left Halifax, Yorkshire in 1636 sailing from Bristol to Boston aboard the "James". One of their descendants, Leonard Butterfield, born in New Hampshire, later became a missionary to the Indians in the Cherokee Valley, North Carolina. When the government took possession of the Indian land in 1838, forcing the tribe to take the now historic "Trail of Tears" joining their old home to the new in Oklahoma, Leonard, his wife and baby accompanied them as far as Tennessee. There they decided to travel north for Griggsville to stay with relatives until they were able to obtain their own land, and build a house. Their son Henry was eventually to farm 150 acres of land nearby. A noted local tenor he married Lydia Adelle Garraux, an accomplished musician and the daughter of a soldier in Napoleon's army. Their cabin was unusual in that it contained Lydia's most prized possession, a Kanabe grand piano. Each of their children learned to play an instrument while Henry, a keen horseman, also taught each of them to ride. In 1891 the Burland and the Butterfield families were united with the marriage of baby William Burland's son, John, to Henry Butterfield's daughter, Ethel.

In the year 2003 the traditions of those far off days are still being upheld. Cleve, Kim and John Curry are the sons of Muriel Curry, grand-daughter of Ethel and John, and her husband, Charles who died in 1984. Between the three of them they now farm some of the original Butterfield, Burland and Bickerdike land on which Muriel still lives. Her life is closely involved with the Church of the Nazarene in Griggsville, two miles away, and as well as working in her home, dressing ducks and chickens, cooking, canning and freezing their own produce which includes strawberries, raspberries, blackcurrants, peaches and grapes, giving cookery demonstrations, helping to look after her grandchildren and doing voluntary work at her local hospital, she also teaches violin and cello. In fact all her pupils, including her own grandchildren, formed a Young Musicians Orchestra which has given many concerts.

The life on the land is busy but satisfying. The three Curry sons, in partnership together, have no outside help. Together they farm more than 3000 acres and each year grow several hundred acres of corn and soya beans plus wheat, alfalfa and some oats. They also have a herd of a hundred and fifty Hereford and Angus cattle, and raise 4000 pigs annually as well as 200 chickens which come as day old chicks from the local hatchery. The cock birds eventually provide fried chicken, the hens eggs for the four families with some left over to sell locally. There are horses for riding and the Curry grandchildren, some of whom now have children of their own, had their own ponies, keeping goats, geese, ducks and guinea fowl for fun.

The trees John and Rebecca knew are of course no more, and the farm now stands on the prairie. Every year the family attends the annual Apple Festival when the horses are hitched to the waggon and everyone takes part in the parade. Griggsville, which in 1983 celebrated the hundred and fiftieth anniversary of its foundation has only 1200 inhabitants and is a "dry" town where alcohol is forbidden. The young people make their own amusements, gathering at each others homes for games such as volleyball and table tennis as well as playing musical instruments. All three Curry sons attended Bethany Nazarene College, Bethany, Oklahoma. A religious colony since 1909, Bethany retains strong religious and moral values where gambling as well as alcohol are forbidden as are dance halls and theatres. Cleve Curry, a talented pianist and violinist met his wife, Suzanne who comes from

Kansas when they were both at College together studying music. In addition to working some of the time on the farm, moving cattle while riding horseback and driving the tractor at harvest time, Susan also plays piano and organ, gives music lessons and teaches English. She and Cleve have four grown up children, Carol Lisa, Rachel, Justin and Sarah.

Kim Curry is a qualified pilot with his own plane which he uses for crop spraying. His wife Lynn who helps on the farm from time to time, is also a hospital voluntary worker and she too gives piano lessons. In 1997 they visited Swillington, Barwick and Thorner where they were warmly welcomed by those people who now live in the old homes of the Burlends and Bickerdikes. Kim and Lynn have two grown-up daughters, Angela and Alicia.

John Curry and his wife, Patty, a hairdresser and beautician, met at their local church, married in 1982 and have two teenage daughters, Diane and Deborah. Patty comes from a local farming family, and like everyone else does her share of the farmwork in addition to running her own business. Besides playing the violin, John's hobby is bee keeping, his hives supplying the family with honey.

Some winters, like the first Rebecca and John experienced, are particularly savage; in 1982 the temperature with wind-chill factors registered 80 degrees below freezing. Each Christmas when the family has received their presents, the horses complete with bells are harnessed to the sleigh and they ride out over the land which John and Rebecca once knew so well but which is now so very different. Success in their adopted country was not attained easily and proved to be the product of a careful blend of ingredients. A judicious choice of land and site, a little capital used prudently, commonsense, resourcefulness, stamina, courage and sheer hard work. By the end of the twentieth century the price of land per acre, originally $1.25 had risen to $2300. Every dollar they earned or had bequeathed to them was swiftly converted into rich land where their virtually unceasing labour combined with heavy rains and intense summer heat created a landscape lush and abundant with crops. There had also of course to be a little luck, especially in the guise of good health. That this was often elusive is borne out by the countless cemeteries all over the mid-west which contain the graves of so many settlers who failed to achieve even half of their normal life span.

It is difficult, if not impossible today for us to have any real appreciation of the circumstances which surrounded John and Rebecca and others like them. Unlike modern emigrants they had no government aid upon which to rely, either for support or for repatriation, and there were no welfare agencies to smooth their path. The few insurance schemes which existed were very much in their infancy, there was no health care, no formal system of education, and although their lives depended totally on the land they owned and the crops they grew, their husbandry was of the most rudimentary. Sophisticated ploughs, harrows, seed drills, harvesters and binders all belonged to the future. They could never have dreamed that one day all these would readily be available to their descendants, and more particularly that one day their great great great grandson would tend his crops from the air!

The many thousands of people like John and Rebecca who came across the sea from every corner of the world, formed the backbone of their new country. They were the basis upon which was built the vast continent which is the modern America. They came to the mid-west with their knowledge and their labour to seek their fortune and their freedom, to start afresh in a land unfettered by its past. For those who survived and prospered, the lush and virgin land generously bestowed upon them that richest of all rewards, a life of liberty and purpose. Some of those settlers, like John and Rebecca, also brought with them their trust in God. It is reassuring to discover that those sound Christian principles and the values in which they believed so implicitly are still the mainstay of close family ties, passed carefully from one generation to the safe-keeping of the next. This, together with the memory of other lands and other times, is still the most cherished legacy of all in the homes of their descendants. More than one hundred and seventy years after their arrival in America, John and Rebecca would be justifiably proud of the huge and happy family which has grown from that precarious foundation they laid so long ago.

Epilogue

THE ORIGINAL pamphlet on which this book is based was 'A True Picture of Emigration, or Fourteen years in the Interior of North America; being a full and impartial account of the various difficulties and ultimate success of an English family who emigrated from Barwick in Elmet near Leeds in the year 1831.' Clearly intended to serve principally as a guide for prospective emigrants, the author had confined himself entirely to the establishment of the family and the first fourteen years in their adopted country. In order to expand the story the first essential was to establish the family's surname to which end I had only five clues. First, in 1817 a woman called Rebecca and her unnamed husband had taken a fourteen year lease on a farm at Barwick in Elmet. Second, in 1831 they had emigrated from Liverpool on a ship called the "Home" which had docked in New Orleans on the 1st November. Third, their ultimate destination had been Pike County, Illinois. Fourth, they had taken with them five children, the eldest being a boy of nine, the youngest a baby boy born in the year of emigration, and fifth, they had left behind in England one son old enough to be a pupil teacher, and a daughter said to be in service with a good family.

As the family had not moved to Barwick until 1817, the two oldest children must have been baptised elsewhere. Therefore in the hope of finding a record of the younger children I began with the baptismal registers of Barwick-in-Elmet. In the late 1970's genealogy was not the popular pastime it has since become, and parish registers were still in the hands of the incumbent who, for a small fee, would conduct a search. It was disappointing, although not too much of a surprise, when this search proved negative. People did not however always attend their nearest church so I therefore widened my options to include every parish church which had existed in the early nineteenth century within a ten mile radius of Barwick. None had a family which matched the details available. A further possibility was that they had belonged to a different religious denomination. Indeed the book stated that for some twenty years prior to her departure for America, Rebecca had been a Wesleyan Methodist although at that time it was unusual for baptisms to be carried out anywhere but in the parish church. There had indeed been a Methodist Chapel in Barwick, and moreover one which dated from the nineteenth century but unfortunately the records were irrevocably lost.

On re-reading the book however I observed that at the end of the preface the author had added, by way of an address, the name of a village 'Swillington' and the date August 1st, 1848. The village of Swillington is on the south eastern outskirts of the city of Leeds, and is small enough to allow for a comprehensive search of the official census of 1841 for a schoolmaster although as this date was some seven years before the publication of the book, there was no guarantee that the author had been living there at that time; in fact the search proved to be relatively simple, revealing just one schoolmaster, name Edward Burland, aged twenty eight, and while the 1841 census does not provide the place of birth of those listed, subsequent ten yearly returns are more detailed. In the returns for 1851 I found the appropriate entry easily.

Edward Burland - aged 38, occupation - schoolmaster, place of birth - Horsforth

Would the parish registers at Horsforth now be able to confirm that Edward's mother was indeed Rebecca? The church at Horsforth, although relatively modern succeeded a previous building, but the baptismal register provided the entry I sought:

"Baptised on the 6th June, 1813, Edward, son of John and Rebecca Burland of Horsforth, farmer" and beneath **"Baptised 26th February, 1815, Mary, daughter of John and Rebecca Burland of Horsforth, farmer"**. .

I now faced a further dilemma. If the two oldest children had been baptised in the Church of England at Horsforth, why had subsequent children not been baptised in the established church at Barwick? A request to re-check the Barwick parish records was turned down, the previous incumbent having by this time moved on. It was however still possible to consult the Bishop's Transcripts, contemporary copies of the registers sent to the appropriate Bishop, and sometimes more complete than the registers themselves. It was there that I found most of the missing Burland children, seven of them in all, the register of burials claiming three in infancy. Of the four remaining there was nine year old John born in 1821, Hannah, Charlotte and Sarah but no sign of William, the baby born in 1831. In fact after legislation had been introduced which required all parish registers to be deposited in local record offices, I was able to examine the Barwick registers for myself and to find most of these entries in the original registers. Somehow they had been overlooked during the initial search, not surprising in view of the fact that I had been unable to provide a surname!

Edward's book had ended with his mother's return to Illinois, and left many queries unanswered. Did the Burlands remain in the United States? If so, did they continue to prosper? What became of their children? Were there indeed descendants still living in the States? I longed to be able to complete the story and began by searching through the telephone directories of every major city in the United States, an exercise which revealed only a handful of Burlands to whom letters produced no useful leads. The next move was therefore to write to The Church of Jesus Christ of Latter Day Saints in Salt Lake City, Utah. The Mormons are the possessors of the most comprehensive collection of genealogical data in the world, and although their computer had no record of the name Burland, a helpful letter suggested that I should contact the Illinois State Historical Society in Springfield, Illinois asking them to insert in their journal an appeal for the descendants of John and Rebecca.

Frankly I held out little hope of success. Any descendants may not have remained in Illinois and even if they had, I felt that the chances of them being sufficiently interested in genealogy to read the quarterly Journal of the Illinois State Historical Society were probably remote. I had not however taken into account the fascination genealogy held and indeed still holds for the American people. In March 1980 I received two letters from Illinois, neither admittedly from Burland descendants, but both expressing interest and giving me addresses and telephone numbers of people who were. Before I was able to contact these people however, I received a letter from Pike County, Illinois. The writer was Muriel Curry, the great great grand-daughter of John and Rebecca, and by a stroke of luck, also the great grand-daughter of William, the baby who had travelled across the Atlantic in his mother's arms. This meant that she was also a descendant of John Bickerdike. Muriel's letter was not only the answer to all my questions; it was also the start of a long and rewarding friendship. From her I discovered that in 1856, Edward Burland had published a second edition of the original pamphlet, presumably in response to the fact that the first edition had sold two thousand copies in Leeds alone, and that this edition had borne the surname that it had taken me so long to discover!

In 1936 the original pamphlet had been discovered by a collector of rare books, Mr. Oliver R. Barrett of Kenilworth, Illinois who like me had set out to identify the family concerned by sifting out of the book all the available biographical information. Unlike me however, Mr. Barrett had the advantage of being able to consult the Illinois land records for the area in which the Burlands first settled, and having learned the surnames of all the settlers from England, he was able to narrow the field further by discovering that only one, John Burland, had had a wife called Rebecca. Further research tended to confirm that he had indeed hit on the true identity of the family, and he accordingly wrote to Mr. Jesse M. Thompson, editor of the Pike County Republican newspaper who had written a series of articles on the history of the county. Mr. Barrett suggested that this family would make another such article, and it was greatly to his surprise when he discovered that Jesse Thompson was in fact a great grandson of John and Rebecca, his grandmother being their youngest daughter, Sarah. All Mr. Barrett's suppositions as to the identity of the family were therefore verified, and his affection for the story subsequently encouraged him to recommend it to the Lakeside Press, publishers of a series of volumes dealing with pioneer life in the American West. The Lakeside Classics edition of "A True Picture of Emigration" appeared in the United States in 1936 in the form of the 1848 edition save that it contained a historical preface by the publishers outlining brief biographical facts as they had been supplied by Oliver Barrett and Jesse Thompson.

Muriel Curry's late mother, Edith, was a keen family historian and from her Muriel had inherited many photographs and items which chronicled the family history. It was Muriel who filled in many of the gaps, who brought me up to date with the family news, who sent me copies of old photographs as well as new ones taken by herself, who photocopied old documents so that I might see them for myself, and who told me so much of the present day lives of the literally hundreds of Burland descendants, many of whom still live in Pike County. Much more than all that however, it was Muriel who welcomed me into her family, who never allowed me to feel intrusive even when I was bombarding her for information and who, by her many friendly and informative letters, gave me so much insight into the lives of the family members today.

The village of Thorner where the story began is no longer as remote from the outside world as it once was. Today the major city of Leeds has crawled across the fields to within a couple of miles of the grey stone cottages and the farm where the Burlands and the Bickerdikes once lived. Thankfully some of the heavier burdens imposed by the twentieth century upon rural communities have been avoided. There has been no reckless demolition and only a little building development but inevitably the old insularity, for better or worse, has gone never to return. So however has poverty and drudgery. The expansion of the city and the advent of the car has converted the village to some extent into commuter country. Two hundred and twenty three years after the birth of John Burland the inhabitants of his birthplace now regard Thorner as a place in which to relax rather than to work, a haven to which they retreat nightly tending immaculate lawns behind lavishly modernised cottages. Today there is no forge in the village and the old school which stood by the church lych gate has been converted into an attractive private house. The sampler which Elizabeth Bickerdike worked while at this school is still in the proud possession of the family and hangs in the home of a descendant in Rockford, Illinois. Across the fields, Carr Farm, home of the Bickerdike family, is still a working farm, while old Nanny's cottage, although derelict and tumbledown, stands forlornly at a turn of the lane. There are however battles to be fought. Residents have to be ever vigilant to keep at bay the speculators and planners who would, if they could, fill in the small but precious acreage between town and country; in 2003 the village finds itself threatened by the incongruous prospect of a municipal cemetery on its doorstep. They must also guard their school where a falling roll of pupils could mean closure, support their village church, preserve their transport service which has to make a detour from the main road in order to serve the village, and if their local shops are to remain open, they require constant patronage. All these amenities contribute to the heart of the village binding it into a cohesive unit, in many ways different from before but still essentially the same, and above all, proud and independent.

The small town of Guiseley where John and Rebecca married has suffered far more in the way of so-called improvements. Now it sprawls across the southern side of a 900 foot ridge called the Chevin which divides the valleys of Wharfedale and Airedale, the former a place of great rural beauty, the latter with many once attractive villages but now very much part of the industrial heart of Yorkshire. Guiseley itself is a small grey manufacturing town whose boundaries are now hard to define with its share of modern shops, housing estates and factories together with a railway which still carries commuters between Wharfedale and the cities of Leeds and Bradford.

Like Thorner, Barwick in Elmet has also undergone change while succeeding in retaining much of its own identity. John and Rebecca's home, still a working farm, stands at the end of the main street, and the old chapel which was opened in 1804 and where Rebecca worshipped remains although it is now used for other purposes. A modern Methodist Church was opened in 1900 as a memorial to the old evangelical preacher, William Dawson, while the school in the churchyard, once attended by the Burland children, was demolished in 1851 and has been replaced by a modern building at the other side of the main street. Sadly there are no Burland memorials in the churchyard for in 1959 many of the headstones were removed in order that ornamental trees may be planted. There is however one survivor from the past in the main street of the village. Every three years on Easter Monday for probably more than one thousand years the eighty seven foot three ton wooden maypole painted red, white and blue has been lowered for maintenance, re-painting and decoration with rosettes before being re-erected by the men of the village on the Tuesday of the Spring Bank Holiday. Sadly however this tradition has recently fallen victim to litigious times, the practice being considered too dangerous; in future a crane may have to be employed in the lowering and raising of the pole - not perhaps exactly as it used to be in the days when John and Rebecca lived in Barwick but at least the tradition still exists - for the present!

Bibliography

Primary sources

West Yorkshire Archives Service Leeds District Archives
Rectory Court Rolls - Thorner 1775-1802
Enclosure Award - Thorner 1777
Parish Registers - Barwick-in-Elmet All Saints 1653-1976
    Guiseley St. Oswald 1585-1975
    Horsforth St. Margaret 1693-1965
    Thorner St. Peter 1622-1948
Estate papers of the Earls of Mexborough

Leeds Central Reference Library
Population Census Returns 1841, 1851, 1861, 1871

The Borthwick Institute of Historical Research, York
Bishop's Transcripts for Barwick-in-Elmet

Wakefield District Library Headquarters.
Parish Registers Sandal Magna St. Helen 1651-1922

National Library of Congress, Washington D.C., U.S.A.
Customs Passenger Lists - New Orleans 1820-1902

History, Directory and Gazetteer of the County of York. Edward
    Baines. 1822
Leeds Intelligencer 1793
Lloyd's Register of Shipping, 1831.

Secondary sources
ALLEN, H. C. Great Britain and the United States (New York, 1955).
ANNESLEY, C.
and HOSKIN, P. Archbishop Drummond's Visitation Returns 1764
    Vol.III, Borthwick Texts & Calendars 26 (York, 2001) p.75.

BACON, F. R. Bacon's Essays: annotated by R. Whateley (London, 1856).

BANTOFT, Arthur 'A Greater Wonder' - a History of Methodism in Barwick. (Barwick-in-Elmet, 1992)

BOGUE, Allan G. From Prairie to Cornbelt (Chicago, 1963).

BRIGGS, Asa A History of England (London, 1967)

BROWN, T. W. The Making of a Yorkshire Village - Thorner (Thorner, 1991).

BRYANT, Sir Arthur The Age of Elegance 1812-1822 (London, 1950).

BURLEND, Edward A True Picture of Emigration, or Fourteen Years in the Interior of North America (London, 1848; second edition 1856).

BURLEND, Edward A True Picture of Emigration Milo Milton Quaife (ed.,) (Chicago,1936; reprinted New York, 1936).

BURLEND, Rebecca, and Edward A True Picture of Emigration Milo Milton Quaife (ed.,) (New York, 1968)

A True Picture of Emigration (Pike County, 1995)

The Wesleyan Emigrants (London, 1856).

Village Rhymes; or Poems on various subjects principally appertaining to incidents in village life, (privately published, 1869).

Amy Thornton, or The Curate's daughter (Leeds, 1863).

BURTON, A. The Rainhill Story (London, 1980).

BUTCHER, Norman The Ancient Parish of Barwick in Elmet (1970)

CANDLER, G. M. The Way West (The American Museum, Bath, Somerset)

COBBETT, William Rural Rides (London, 1979)

COLEMAN, Terry Passage to America (Newton Abbott, 1973).

ERICKSON, Charlotte Invisible Immigrants (London, 1972).

ERNLE, R. E. M. English farming past and present (London, 1912).

FARAGHER, J. M. Women and men on the overland trail (New Haven, 1979).

Sugar Creek: life on the Illinois Prairie (New Haven and London, 1986.

FURNAS, J. C. The Americans: a social history of the United States 1587-1914 (London, 1970).

HANSEN, M. L The Atlantic Migration 1607-1860 (Cambridge, Mass., 1945).

HAVIGHURST, W. Wilderness for sale (New York, 1956).

The Heartland: Ohio, Indiana and Illinois (New York & Evanstone, 1956).

HOBSON, R. P., Jr. Grass beyond the Mountains (Toronto, 1951).

JOHNSON, S. C. A History of Emigration from the United Kingdom to North America 1763-1912 (London, 1913).

JONES, M. A. Destination America (London, 1976).

American Immigration (Cambridge, 1960).

KIRK, G. E. A Short History of the Parish Church of St. Peter, Thorner (1935).

McLAUGHLIN, R. The Heartland (New York, 1967).

ROBINSON, H. Carrying British Mails overseas (London, 1964).

ROYLE, E. Modern Britain: a social history 1750-1985 (London, 1989).

SMITH, A. H. The Place Names of the West Riding of Yorkshire English Place Names Society Vol. XXXIII (Cambridge, 1961).

TREVELYAN, G. M. English Social History (London, 1948).

TREVELYAN, G. M. British History in the Nineteenth Century and after: 1782-1919 (London, 1979).

WATSON, J. S. The Reign of George III, 1760-1815 (Oxford, 1960).

WOODWARD, Sir L. The Age of Reform, 1815-1870 (Oxford, 1962).

Genealogy

THE FAMILY TREE has been compiled from a combination of parish registers, Bishop's transcripts, memorial inscriptions, census returns and family recollection, and is as accurate as these sources allow. It is very far from being complete, but it is hoped that sufficient information has been provided to set the family in context without confusing the reader.

There is no record of William in the Barwick-in-Elmet baptismal register. However as he was born on the 24th May, 1831 and the family left Barwick in the last week of August, perhaps John and Rebecca were too preoccupied with their imminent departure coinciding as it did with a particularly busy time in the farming calendar. Nor is there any record in either the baptismal, or for that matter the burial, registers of Harriet and Maria. They do however appear in the Bishop's transcripts - sometimes more complete than the registers - of the burials for Barwick. Presumably they were either stillborn, or died before baptism.

Although the American, and indeed some of the English members of the family, to-day spell their surname **Burlend**, most of the primary sources relating to the family in England use the form **Burland.** In order to avoid misquoting these sources, I have therefore adhered to the latter spelling.

Thomas Burland=1719 **Sarah Robinson**
1697-1745   -1746
issue - 2 daughters
     1 son

Stephen Burland =1750 **Hannah Dixon**
1720-1797   1721-1790
issue - 4 sons

Edward Burland =1781 **Mary Marsden**
1755-1835   1759-1833
issue - 3 daughters
     5 sons

John Burland =1811 **Rebecca Burton**
1783-1871   1793-1872
issue - 8 daughters
     4 sons

William Burland=1856 **Elizabeth Bickerdike**
1831-1900   1828-1910
issue - 4 daughters
     3 sons

John Burland=1891 **Ethel Butterfield**
1862-1930   1872-1942
issue - 2 sons
     1 daughter

Edith Burland=1918 **John Myers**
1896-1977   1894-1985
issue - 1 daughter

Muriel Myers=1946 **Charles Curry**
               1925 -1984
issue - 3 sons

Notes

1 L. Woodward, The Age of Reform (Oxford, 1979), p.601.
2 J. S. Watson, The Reign of George III 1760-1815 (Oxford, 1976), p.39.
3 Quoted in A. Briggs, A History of England (London, 1967), p.67.
4 R. E. Ernle, English Farming Past and Present (London, 1912), p.264.
5 West Yorkshire Archive Service, Leeds, Enclosure Award for Thorner 1777.
6 T. W. Brown, The Making of a Yorkshire Village - Thorner (Thorner, 1991) pp.74;76.
7 York Faculty Book 2 cited in Brown, p.81.
8 C. Annesley & P. Hoskin, Archbishop Drummond's Visitation Returns 1764, Vol. III Borthwick Texts and Calendars 26 (York, 2001), p.75.
9 Faculty Book cited in Brown, p.81.
10 Leeds Intelligencer, February 1793.
11 Brown, Thorner, p.96.
12 Ledsham Church, Lady Mary Bolles (pamphlet-author unknown) , Extracts from Will 1662, pp.5-6.
13 Ernle, English Farming, etc., p.273.
14 M. M. Quaife (ed.,), Rebecca and Edward Burlend, A True Picture of Emigration (New York, 1968), p.7.
15 A. H. Smith (ed.,), The Place Names of the West Riding of Yorkshire, Part IV, Vol. XXXIII (Cambridge, 1961), p.106.
16 J. Simon (ed.,), State of Humanity, 1993.
17 A. Bantoft, 'A Greater Wonder - a history of Methodism in Barwick (Barwick-in-Elmet, 1992) pp.1-2.
18 E. Burlend, A True Picture of Emigration (2nd edit.), (Leeds, 1856), p.199.
19 A. Burton, The Rainhill Story (London, 1980), p.154.
20 Lloyd's Register of Shipping, 1831.
21 G. M. Candler, The Way West (Bath - undated) p.8.
22 E. Royle, Modern Britain: a social history 1750-1985 (London, 1989), p.63.
23 4 Geo. 4, c.83; 6 Geo. 4, c.116.
24 5 & 6 W. 4, C.53, s.13.
25 43 Geo. 3, c.56.
26 5 & 6 W. 4, c.53, s. 3, 4.
27 Candler, The Way West, pp.13-14.
28 ibid., p. 26.
29 ibid., p.22.
30 W. Havighurst, Wilderness for Sale (New York, 1956), p.45.
31 A. G. Bogue, From Prairie to Cornbelt (Chicago, 1968), pp.30-31.
32 Quaife, A True Picture, etc., p.57.
33 Bogue, From Prairie, etc., p.148.
34 Burlend, A True Picture, etc., p.81.
35 J. M. Faragher, Sugar Creek (New Haven and London, 1986), pp.89-90.
36 Bogue, From Prairie, etc., pp.31-39.